Guidance From Within

You Can Have a Conversation With God

Guidance From Within

You Can Have a Conversation With God

Ernest F. Pecci, M.D.

Transformational Concepts Brought To Life

Pavior Publishing
Walnut Creek California

ISBN: 1-929331-06-1

Library of Congress Control Number: 2003093473

Library of Congress Cataloging-in-Publication Data

Pecci, Ernest F.
 Guidance from within : you can have a conversation with God / Ernest F. Pecci.
  p. cm.
Includes index.
 ISBN 1-929331-06-1 (alk. paper)
 1. Mental health—Religious aspects. 2. Psychiatry and religion. 3. Spiritual life. I. Title.
 BL65.M45 P43 2003
 291.1'78322—dc21
                                        2003010982

Pavior Publishing
Walnut Creek, California

If you are unable to order this book from your local bookseller you may order directly from our website www.pavior.com

Dedication

To all of my teachers
who came to me as patients,
to ask me to explain to them what I needed to learn.

Acknowledgments

Special thanks is due to those people who were willing to share their own personal writings in this book and most of whoms names have been changed in the text to respect their privacy.

Special acknowledgement to Joanne Walsh whose encouragement, questioning, editing, and personal contributions were of especially valuable to me in the production of this book.

And, finally, special recognition must be given to Robert Sheppie who, inspired by his wife Shelly, was responsible for the final formatting and design of this book including the cover artwork.

Table of Contents

A Personal Invitation
Preface

Part I

CHAPTER 1

CHAPTER 2

CHAPTER 3

CHAPTER 4

Part II

CHAPTER 5

CHAPTER 6

Part III

This section contains aphorisms, affirmations and reinforcement of the essential truths in the earlier chapters of this book. Turn to it when you need an emotional lift or encouragement to shift your thoughts to feel more positive about your life.

CHAPTER 7

A Personal Invitation

Perhaps you have been seeking, but you haven't known where to look, or exactly what it was you were looking for. Most people are not entirely satisfied with the way their lives are working, but don't know what to do about it. Many seekers struggle long and with great intensity, but answers continue to elude them. It was your seeking that has led you to this book. This is the first of several books that can open the door to a life that is like a fairy tale, one like Cinderella or the ugly duckling who became a beautiful swan. With the willingness you now have, very small steps can slowly bring gratifying results. Let me share with you the kinds of questions that have been brought to me during my forty years of practice.

The times are chaotic, confusing, demanding, and often frightening. Most people I know are out of sync with themselves and with each other. And I don't even have time to do what is essential, let alone time to find inner peace—if there is such a thing. What do I have to do to find it?

What you need is a source of guidance that brings a sense of security with the reassurance that something bigger than yourself is running the universe and can be trusted to do what will ultimately be for your own benefit. Our conscious Intellect is only a small speck of that vast expanse that comprises our total consciousness. Our goal is not only that of reaching a state of inner peace, but of living life fully. Continual change is a necessary part of the process of growth. But you no longer have to face new experiences with fear if you know that loving guidance is always available.

I could really use guidance. Protection? I need that too. I feel so cut off from everything and, often, from everyone. I don't know where I am supposed to be going and what matters. If I decide I have a strong passion for something, could I be guided to really satisfy it?

There is no greater sense of protection than feeling connected to your Creator, and no greater fear than when that connection seems lost. Your true heart's desire was intended to be happily fulfilled. When you begin to question whether you really know what it is that will satisfy you, you are most open to guidance. Most people are too busy to notice or to recognize the many "clues" or nudges that gently prod them in the direction they should be going.

How can this book help me to find this guidance you are referring to?

There are basically three types of information, as alluded to by the Russian mystic and philosopher, Gurdjieff. You are undoubtedly well acquainted with the first two: type "A" is academic information such as taught in our educational system, and type "B" consists of practical information for relating to others and handling the problems of survival in the world. These are the types of information that are contained in many self-help books. The accumulation of types "A" and "B" information leads to knowledge about the outer world that is necessary for attaining degrees, status, and a profitable livelihood. There is no limit to the availability of new information that you can study to expand your intellectual base of knowledge in a horizontal fashion. *However, there is no direct correlation between your accumulation of these types of information and your level of happiness and freedom from problems.*

Then there is type "C" information that results in a vertical growth in consciousness and makes you a witness, from a higher perspective, of the real meaning of your everyday activities. It helps you to understand and to experience who and what you are, to discover your life purpose, and to obtain the vast unseen resource at your disposal to guide and assist you to the successful completion of that purpose. This book teaches you how to obtain type "C" information.

What is this "unseen resource" of which you speak?

We don't even have a vocabulary for that supernatural force beyond the five senses that is reaching out more strongly today than ever before to prepare us for a major jump in evolution. I refer to it in this book as the voice of the Helper. It is your own higher or knowing Self, indistinguishable from what you now call "God." It is free from the mind of your little self that is held hostage by social customs, parental rules, past conditioning and fixed beliefs. Your learning until now has often been in disagreement with your own inner truth. As a result, you are constantly making decisions as to when to conform or not to conform to the rules that the world imposes upon you. This keeps your mind in conflict and confusion. A confused mind cannot heal itself, but it can listen to the voice of the Helper that is constantly trying to guide you.

I don't know what to ask God, and I'm not sure I want to know His answers, even if I could reach Him.

When you reach out to the Source of Love, nothing you have been or done will bring judgment, disapproval, or punishment. This book will help you to ask for the acceptance, caring, knowing, and guidance that you have always wanted. Most people are concerned with the basic issues of survival, security, being accepted and gaining respect or praise from others. If we felt secure with these issues, life would be far less difficult and stressful. The ultimate goal of all questioning is to align your outer personality with your inner truth, which is to say, to become one with your Soul.

Is there really a way, without years of major therapy or long, deep inner work to truly feel understood and still loved? I want to have some sense of significance. I want to feel that my being on earth has made a positive difference to someone or something! Is this possible?

Yes. For all of your uncertainty and your struggling with the meaning and the value of life here on earth, feeling significant and loved unconditionally would change your feelings about absolutely everything else. And reaching that feeling may be much easier than you believe.

All of my life I have been taught about the unapproachableness of God – unless I am on my knees in supplication. Is it appropriate for me to expect that God will talk to me personally?

What have you to lose by discovering this for yourself? You can always evaluate the efficacy of the material you receive. You can begin by writing about a problem on paper – and then elect to receive an answer. You may be surprised to discover that the answer contains ideas, perspectives, and possibilities not expected or previously expressed through your thoughts. How do we explain a "hunch," "intuition" or "precognitive dreams?" We may use them, yet not understand exactly how they occur. Through what process and by what means do such things occur? We may not agree on possible explanations. Yet the ideas, the perspectives do occur – and can be used for your benefit.

This book is primarily about writing to God. I have a strong resistance to putting words to paper. Are there any other modes to contact God?

God is constantly reaching out to you on both conscious and unconscious levels in ways that cannot be adequately captured in words, so you may begin with any mode that helps you to know that you have His attention. All that is really needed is the desire and the willingness to quiet your mind and to listen. Some people prefer typing or using a tape recorder. Writing helps to focus your mind, to clarify your thoughts, and to find words to define your questions. But many have shared with me the comforting experience of talking to God even while driving their car to work. Soon you will notice that instant answers are always available whenever you find yourself in an emotional predicament and take the time to pause to ask for help. The dialogue is continuous.

How do I know that I am talking to God and not just to myself to make myself feel good?

Even that could be helpful. However, It is much like dialing a telephone. Your mind eventually succeeds in reaching the level it is seeking. It has a special quality and feeling to it. You will usually be impressed when you read your words the next day. The tone of the words is often different from your usual writing style, and the ideas expressed are not ones that would ordinarily occur to you.

Can I really expect the quality of my life to be enhanced by writing to God? Would I be able to use the advice? Wouldn't it be difficult to change my old patterns? Can I really do it?

Your *willingness* to change old beliefs is the only beginning you need. You have probably already discovered that old habits and beliefs are like addictions. Even your determined resolutions are not strong enough to change them without Higher help. But as you begin to see positive results, it becomes easier and easier to open yourself up to a new way of thinking.

I want to believe that such a wonderful connection is available to me and that it can improve my life. What would that be like?

We don't know the ultimate possibilities of this thing we call "life." Once it was thought that a man could not run a mile in 4 minutes. Then someone named Roger Bannister did it. After that "barrier" was broken, more and more athletes achieved the same feat – until the running time was reduced even further on a regular basis. Neale Walsch in his first book, <u>A Conversation With God</u>, may well have broken a "barrier" that only waits for the next writer, and maybe even you. What have you to lose but your little self, and to gain, except your true Self, with its unlimited potentiality?

Please explain to me the benefit of my seriously deciding to do this?

You can ease stress and bring harmony into your life by becoming a loving being. Loving must come from a state of wholeness and self-acceptance in all situations. Then life can become a joyful adventure, and also a gratifying sharing that brings equal benefit to others.

You have my interest, but it is still hard to believe that life was meant to be a joyful adventure. Can I really find a way to make my life work?

Do you have the wish to believe that there is something more, and the will to persevere until you find it?

Are you willing to see things differently, even when it means admitting that many of your fixed beliefs must be changed?

Are you determined, now, to embrace the inner feelings that you suppressed as a child and to behave in a new way, even when change is sometimes associated with fear?

Are you ready to listen to another voice that is far gentler and wiser than all the other voices that now fill your head?

Notice how the universe works in perfect harmony. Your free will has allowed you to break away from that harmony. It was for a purpose, to provide a unique experience that you agreed upon before your birth in order to enrich your Soul's growth in ways that you cannot now imagine. Something inside of you is now making you more restless as time passes, and is urging you to listen to the inner voice that will guide you back into the natural stream of universal energy and with the flow of all life.

Ernest F. Pecci, MD

Preface

The field of psychiatry deals with the emotional pain, doubt, guilt, fears, and remorse associated with the problems of living. For the vast majority of people on this planet, life is difficult, life is stressful, and life is synonymous with worry and pain even for those who do not seek help. The work of a psychiatrist is often tedious because of the built-in resistances that everyone has, to a greater or lesser extent, against changing their old, dysfunctional but familiar patterns of behavior. Change usually comes slowly and after considerable effort on the part of both the seeker and the helper. But even then, problems seem to be an integral part of life, and feelings of stress and depression are on the increase because of the growing complexity of our social structure, relationships, work pressures and financial stress, even in affluent societies.

Despite amazing advances in science and technology, most people are not feeling freer and happier. In fact, over the past thirty years the general population is using an increasing number of medications and mind-altering substances just to tolerate their existence.

From the beginning of my practice of psychiatry, I often asked myself, "What do I really have to offer the people who come to me for answers to their problems?" Their options, on the surface, appeared so limited. They felt trapped in the web of their environment and by their need to conform to the expectations of others who were important to them. Often they were torn between feeling happy or feeling guilty.

Real happiness appears to be rare or, at best, fleeting. For most, it requires a constant effort just to maintain a basic sense of stability and security. Certainly, the opinion of a caring counselor can offer some reassurance and comfort. But to what end? Is there an ultimate goal or purpose to our life? And is it possible to reach a permanent place of peace, a place in consciousness where everything works?

Frequently I found myself asking, as did Karl Jung a half century before: "What is the secret of the whole person?" Sigmund Freud was instrumental in bringing the Western world to an awareness of how our subconscious mind determines much of our behavior. Is there a superconscious mind as well that governs our destiny and gives a purpose to our life? If so, how can we cooperate with it instead of being in constant conflict with it? Einstein believed there was a God who maintained order in the universe. If so, does that God know about our struggles to survive and does He care? Can we reach Him? Will He respond? Recently, the general public appears to be more willing to accept this possibility as evidenced by the interest in the first of three books by Neale Walsch, <u>A Conversation With God.</u> I would like to share, in this book, my attempts to help others to establish their own personal connection to God, and how this has contributed to significant improvement in the quality of their lives.

The practice of psychiatry has offered me a fertile field of study over the past forty years. I have always believed that, behind exterior appearances, there are powerful forces at work to give meaning and purpose to all of life's experiences. If there are laws that govern every action in the universe, why not laws that govern the actions of humans as well? If we assume that there are no meaningless problems, then the symptoms that patients bring to me offer clues to these unseen forces working through them. Events that appear to be tragic may be necessary to evoke in us the emotional energies needed to push us to the next step up the ladder of evolution. Serious illnesses often lead to a spiritual crisis in which the patient begins asking new questions about life's purpose and meaning. Similarly, the pain we may suffer during a traumatic childhood is not necessarily wasted. It forces us to ask questions that we might not otherwise have asked, and to seek answers at levels we might not have otherwise acknowledged.

People are afraid of emotions because they believe that emotions bring pain. But more pain results from the suppression of emotions. Emotions are the language of the Soul. They add richness and color to our lives and are the source of our happiness. Even emotions that arise from traumatic memories of the past can be useful if seen from a higher level that brings a more complete understanding of their potential usefulness.

I have observed that each individual has a distinct, repetitive life pattern of trauma which, when examined, gives clues as to the lessons that he or she has come here to learn in order to grow. We miss these opportunities to grow when we accept our being left with nothing more than guilt or blame. The discovery of powerful psychotropic medications over the past few decades has been a blessing to many people. These should not be used solely for symptom relief but as a support to face each life experience to its limit, to drain every ounce of meaning from it, and to come to the realization that despite whatever else happens the Core Self remains intact.

Psychology in the Western world is little more than one hundred years old, while consciousness and the mind have been a focus of study for over 2500 years in the Eastern world. Yet, each has something to offer the other in coming from different directions. In the West, for example, progress is being rapidly made, not only in the development of more effective psychotropic medications, but also in biological and clinical research that demonstrates the interconnectedness between the mind and the body.

Over the past ten years, the psychiatric literature has reported an increasing number of clinical studies supporting the dramatic positive value that holding an intrinsic belief in a higher power can have upon maintaining mental and physical health. Here is a list of just a few of these findings:

> "Adults over 50 years of age who hold religious beliefs are four times less likely to commit suicide than those who do not."

"People with a high level of religious conviction are less likely to become involved in substance abuse."

"Religious teens are less likely to carry weapons, get into fights, or engage in promiscuous sex."

"Religious belief increases the rate of cure and decreases the incidence of depression."

"Almost 90% of alcoholics report that they had lost interest in religion during their teenage years."

"Elderly patients with strong religious beliefs are much more likely to survive serious medical procedures including heart surgery."

Intrinsic spiritual beliefs can increase our receptivity to help from higher sources. Each person has latent within every cell of his or her body an "antenna system" connected to the universal matrix of all knowing. This is closed down by our educational and cultural influences that focus upon our Intellect, which is limited to the five senses. Dr. William Tiller, professor emeritus at Stanford University, verifies these antenna systems in his groundbreaking book, <u>Science and Human Transformation</u>, (Pavior Publishing, 1997) in which he mathematically bridges the gap between subtle energy phenomena such as extrasensory perception with the scientifically accepted facts of the Western world.

The exercises in this book are based upon a premise of utmost importance, namely the existence of a higher level of conscious awareness that, in comparison to the consciousness of humanity, warrants the label of "God." Furthermore, that this "God" is mindful and caring of humans, and that humans have the capacity to contact and to receive guidance directly from this Source. We might be able to avoid a philosophical argument by treating the concept of God as we treat electricity. We don't have to know what electricity really is in order to use it. And when we learn to use it, we accept that it must exist.

The time has come to seek higher-level solutions to our complex problems. Our society breeds loneliness and a sense of depersonalization. Our adolescents suffer from an undefined feeling of God hunger. Rapidly occurring changes are challenging our Intellect for answers regarding ourself and our purpose. We are witnessing the fall of the past structures of authority that we once turned to for answers. This is creating a need to turn to our own self for truth. Our youth, our middle-aged working class, and our senior citizens are questioning more than ever the meaning and purpose of their lives. The old answers are not enough. Our family structure and support systems are breaking down. This has resulted in an increase in depression and anxiety, a lack of direction, a loss of meaning, and an increase in new medical syndromes such as chronic fatigue and fibromyalgia. Generalized anxiety and panic attacks have become a common cause for seeking help at every age level.

On the positive side, all of this is forcing us to progressively diminish our reliance upon outer authority and to turn within, to fall back upon our Core Self that is now covered by the superficial trappings of the external world.

The information explosion and the growth in technology, instead of improving our way of life, are leading to a destruction of our planet, the pollution of our atmosphere, and to the increasing complexity of our lives. Where else can we turn for peace, nurturance, and the assuring support once provided by family and friends? The answer lies in a closer examination of the questions: "Who am I?" "What is my connection to the Universe, and to what end?" "Is there a God, and does He/She really care about me?"

In recent years there has been a revival within the general population of seekers for answers from a higher level. Some of these seekers are led to self-proclaimed teachers and religious sects that claim to have all of the answers. But words that reach the Intellect from outside oneself, no matter how intriguing or sweetly couched, remain superficial and keep the seeker tantalized but incompletely satisfied. You need not travel to far countries to hear the words of famous teachers and gurus when God is everywhere, and the Truth resides within yourself.

We need to learn to listen to the inner voice, which comes as both thoughts and feelings that reach deep to the core of our asking. Karl Jung talked about doing this and called the indwelling Self whom he contacted, "Philemon," the wise old one within." You too can experience this Indwelling Self to lift your spirits and alter your life for the better.

Bringing your questions to God, with the expectation of receiving an answer, opens a channel of which you have, thus far, been unaware. Your skill in its use grows with time. Some people have a resistance to writing and may use other methods of asking and receiving, but nothing retains the storehouse of information that you will receive better than maintaining a daily dialogue. The simple exercises in this book can bring about a change in your life that is difficult to fully explain, but not as difficult to experience as you might think.

PART I

Is There Anybody Out There?

Teaching My Patients To Write To God

Ways In Which God Can Help

Patient Contributions

1

Is There Anybody Out There?

This is not a book of philosophy. It is a book of shared experiences that can lift your spirits and alter your life for the better. The terms "God," "Higher Self," "Higher Mind," and "Inner Being" are used interchangeably here. Any attempt to define God always creates an artificial model because we humans cannot possibly understand God. Nevertheless, despite the limitations of our intellectual understanding, we can still experience Him (or Her or It) as fully as our receptivity will allow. The voice of the indwelling Self is usually very faint and can only be heard with focused attention and desire. This is so because It will not interfere with our free will. Thus it can easily be over-ridden by the Intellect. But practice can help you to more clearly attune your thoughts to what the Bible alludes to as the "Holy Spirit," the "Helper," and the "Good Shepherd."

Consider the premise that you must have had a Creator. What is the nature of your Creator? Certainly you did not create yourself. Neither did your parents create you, although your mother's womb was the receptacle for your miraculous birth. "Who is man that God would be mindful of him?" Would a Creator be expected to be mindful of His Creations? "Who am I?" is as profound a question as "What is God?" Buddha stated that all of our questioning has no useful meaning if it does not help us to come closer to the truth of "Who am I?" "From whence have I come?" and "Where am I going?"

Here is an image that may help to simplify the nature of your Soul and its relationship to God. If you broke an egg into a large frying pan, you would see a yolk surrounded by a large area of white albumin. The yolk is like the physical body, while the white albumin represents the much broader part of the mind that covers but is not confined within the yolk. If we put many eggs into the frying pan, there would be many yolks surrounded by a large "sea" of white. In this way, we are all separate, yet united. And it is this larger, unseen part of ourselves that contains the wisdom of our united Higher Mind.

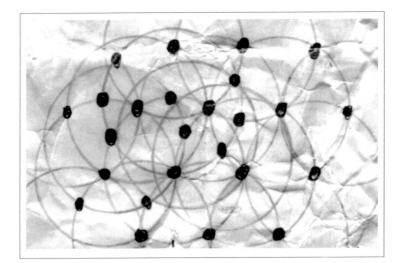

Humanity is like billions of egg yolks in a collective sea of all knowing and all potentialities.

Within this "Higher Mind" each Soul is interconnected and has access to the wisdom of every other Soul past, present, and future. This represents the Sonship or "Son of God" divided into billions of seemingly individual Souls. Your own Soul is a part of a much larger, broader multidimensional Being that is invisible to the naked eye. The little speck of yourself becomes closed off from the rest of your greater, broader Self when in physical form, and especially when you put up a defensive wall of fear. Your "Higher Self" or "Higher Mind" will not break through your defenses unless you ask for help. The more you ask, the more the Intellect stands aside and the wider the channel for help becomes.

According to the ancient teachers, we are all part of the unseen multidimensional matrix that consists of Consciousness-Essence-Being. We are a ray of that Being, which we might refer to as "God," projected upon the plane of earth for a specific experience to serve a higher purpose. Just as white light that splits as it passes through a quartz crystal into a myriad of colors that can be used to create an infinite number of beautiful scenes or paintings, so billions of Souls, like beams of light, radiate out from God's consciousness to engage in an infinite variety of experiences on many planes of existence, and to ultimately return back to their Source. There are also intermediary teachers or guides assigned to every one of us to specifically aid us in the fulfillment of our unique purpose.

Out of the field of quantum physics have emerged startling formulas that indicate that there is far more energy in every square centimeter of "empty" space than in the objects we see with our naked eyes. There also appears to be a definite but inexplicable connection between every human being and every particle in space, so that each person's experience has a ripple effect upon everyone else regardless of distance.

Our physical brain is a biological computer that receives input from the five senses. Our Intellect tries to give meaning to the thin thread of reality it perceives from the very limited data that it receives. But intellectual knowledge cannot begin to find the answers to our deepest questions. Neither has the "information explosion" of the twentieth century in science and technology succeeded in increasing to any significant degree our state of happiness or sense of security.

Historically there has been a tendency for people to turn to other "more learned" people for answers. The inability to make decisions and the fear of taking responsibility has repeatedly allowed the masses to be manipulated in ways that do not serve their own best interests. As a child, your desire to earn love from the authorities that raised you by resonating to their energies and their belief systems was extremely powerful. In later life, there is still much doubt and dread in deviating from this external authority and shifting to the highest authority that resides within your own Self. It is a common aspect of human life to feel isolated or separated. Most people are afraid that others will respond to their being different with disrespect or contempt. And being *nothing* in the eyes of someone is even worse than being *bad* in the eyes of someone. But all Souls are held in equal regard in God's eyes.

The Nature of Your Higher Self

Try to imagine your Higher Self as part of your mind that goes far beyond your physical body. The small segment of your mind that has been drawn to your physical body is in a state of sleep, and your Higher Mind is constantly ready to reach and to awaken your sleeping self. Your Higher Self is the total Self, multidimensional and containing all memory and connectivity to God. It projects a portion of Itself into the earth plane as a physical being with loss of memory but not loss of continuous contact. This permits a sense of independence from God that allows the use of "free will" in making choices toward or away from Him. In all of the sacred teachings, references can be found clearly indicating that God wants to make contact with us. He waits patiently for that time when we are tired of our struggling with "good" and "evil" and finally desire above everything else to return Home. This can only occur after we reach the realization that love is all that we really want, and that loving one another is the only way out of the dream of physical existence. Thus, the 3-dimensional experience is primarily one in which we agreed to become disconnected and to learn by exercising our free will to reconnect.

A sense of loneliness and isolation occurs when a person drifts away from the higher knowing that resides in the center of his being. Thus some pain, deprivation, and mistakes are an inherent part of the journey. No person is left without guides on the higher levels who are constantly urging the right choices and helping to show the right direction leading back to "Home." Your life is being guided on a higher level to bring to you all that is needed. You can dramatically speed up the process by learning to pay attention. The Higher Self can be of immense assistance in offering a new interpretation of how life might be used to serve a higher purpose and lead to psychological growth, new awareness, and happiness. Inner discomfort is a sign that we are not in synch with our Soul's purpose and that we need to re-examine the origins of our beliefs.

It is the desire of the Higher Self to ease pressures, stress, and insecurities that stand in the way of moving on in consciousness. It may inspire you with a desire to write, or an exiting new idea to explore, or an impulse to do something of value to others. These feelings are usually brief and can be easily overridden by the Intellect unless you are prepared to take advantage of the opportunity that is offered. It was never intended, neither is it possible, that humans be cut off from this Source, despite their common feeling of isolation and loneliness. Now is the time to begin asking and listening. There is nothing too menial to request to make one's life smooth and enjoyable. Growth necessitates a gradual change in your belief system. Everything you experience originates from your thoughts. Most of these are not your real thoughts, but the thoughts of authority figures that were imposed upon you in childhood. This lifetime presents a challenge to listen to your own inner truth aside from your social milieu.

The acceptance of a Higher Self includes the expectation that it is available for even the most mundane of activities. Expect your Higher Self to guide you in such simple things as opening a can of soup. It is available to help you in your everyday life in making decisions, solving problems, and finding the things that you are looking for. It can lead you to the right place, the right store, and the right friends. It reacts with every aspect of your minutia of daily living as well as the grandeur of spiritual revelation.

The effort in the beginning can be small and gentle, yet bring about profound changes. Every circumstance of your body and mind can be substantially improved. Whenever a physical discomfort or uncomfortable circumstance arises say, "This exact situation can be much improved." Energies can be changed no matter what their present state, and despite all attack and negativity from others. You can halt negative feelings in the midst of negative circumstances. Somewhere there are answers that will lead to improvement. The mind cannot be open to receiving these answers until you make statements to release the pressure, such as: "This too shall pass." Then expect new doors to open. At the first quiet moment, sit quietly and contemplate. "What should I write as the perfect ending?" This can begin to align and set up energies you need to receive and to alleviate your current sense of off-centeredness. It is also a wonderful exercise to have your children do.

All children, because of their sense of limitation and their vulnerability to abuse are preoccupied, consciously and unconsciously, with three basic questions.

The Three Basic Questions:

> **1.) <u>Am I Safe?</u>** Can I trust that there is a safe degree of acceptance here? Will I be treated favorably without the danger of verbal or physical abuse, embarrassment, or exposure of my weaknesses?

> **2.) <u>Can I Cope?</u>** What will be expected of me? Will I be able to handle whatever comes up? Will I be able to maintain a good front?   Can I consistently meet expectations, make a good impression and be respected?

> **3.) <u>Who Am I?</u>** Am I valued? Am I accepted and wanted? Am I someone important, significant, and loved in this setting?

In my consultations with elementary school teachers, I always emphasized that unless a child has satisfactory answers to all of these questions, no new learning can take place. Unfortunately, because of the very complex and competitive world we live in, most adults are also concerned with these same three questions, which commonly consume a considerable amount of their energies. Their answers to these questions often vary significantly in different situations. The Intellect tries to find the comfort zone. This is what motivates many people to gravitate to a small, safe comfort zone of friends and activities and into a mechanical routine that greatly limits their lives and their relationships.

Expressing openly your fears can generate energy toward change. It is helpful to express fear or anguish, even by writing it on paper. "Is there anybody up there who can help?" If done properly there will be a feeling of release in the belly, even after accepting the worse possible scenario. Once you totally surrender to the situation, an answer will usually come within days in a variety of ways:

1. Meeting a person who can help.
2. Suddenly sensing what action to take.
3. A change in attitude.
4. New and improved circumstances begin to arise.

You may have doubts about your ability to achieve a satisfying, purposeful life experience. Your life may seem complex. You may feel as though you are on a roller coaster ride or an endlessly repetitive merry-go-round. But if you knew that you had a Higher Wisdom that was guiding the complexities of your life, and that you could make a conscious connection to this Higher level of assistance, you could experience it all with a much greater sense of comfort. Even though you cannot feel all the loving energies of the invisible forces working within and around you, a greater acceptance and trust in the universe will greatly reduce your anxiety. If you could read the final chapter of the compendium of books that is "Your Life" and could see the potential for an unbelievably happy ending, wouldn't that help you to experience this present moment differently?

Questioning can gradually open up communication, receptivity, and trust. With this will come a sense of safety, guidance, and increased self-worth. You will begin to believe that your life has meaning and purpose beyond all of your previous expectations. Reading the personal experiences shared in this book of many others who were initially skeptical will help to encourage you to take the first step to initiate communication for yourself.

2

Teaching My Patients To Write To God

After the public acceptance of Neale Walsch's first book, <u>A Conversation With God,</u> I felt that the time had come to teach my patients that it is not as difficult to communicate with God as most people might believe. Most of my patients already had some belief in a higher power. They were raised by parents with a variety of religious beliefs, but very few attended church on a regular basis. I prefaced my instructions to them with a brief discussion of the possibility that our consciousness is somehow linked to the same consciousness that runs the larger universe and that a little willingness was all that was needed to make a personal connection. The results, from the beginning, were far more rewarding than I had expected. I was surprised by what the average person was capable of doing when encouraged in the proper way. Following is the routine that I found to be most helpful:

1. Sit in a comfortable chair with writing materials resting upon a table in front of you.

2. Close your eyes and use whatever technique you know to enter into a relaxed state, such as deep slow breathing or picturing a peaceful natural setting. The intent is to slow down your heart and empty your head from the busy "taped" thoughts that your brain is continually playing, and which

is sometimes labeled, "the inner dialogue." To allow truth to enter your head from your Higher Self, you must quiet conscious thinking, and learn to listen with a clear head and a neutral attitude. All that is required is sincerity, desire, receptivity, and enough faith to give God a chance.

3. Contemplate, from this relaxed state, an issue or challenge facing you today, and take time to slowly formulate one or two clear questions about it. Then write these questions down, prefacing them to: "God," "Higher Self," or whatever title appeals the most to you. Just the letter "Q." for "question" can be sufficient.

4. From your level of questioning, it often seems as if there isn't any easy solution to your problem. However, a seemingly simple answer may direct your thinking to a new level of questioning that raises your awareness to a higher sense of clarity regarding your problem. Life is analogous to a high-tech computer game in which you continually find yourself in new situations and must keep searching for clues to test your options in order to be able to move forward in the right direction. It is certainly much easier when you have guidance and continuous support to find the right answers. Are you willing to hear something new that will alter the attitude that you had the last time you were faced with this same or similar problem in the past?

5. Mentally assume an open-mind and a questioning attitude: "Is there another way of seeing this?" "What am I supposed to be learning?" "What belief about this makes it seem so difficult?" "What is it I really need to know?" When you finally arrive at a meaningful question regarding your situation or feeling of discomfort you will sense it. Write as many sentences as you like about it.

6. Then, skip down a couple of lines and write the letter: "A." for "answer." Briefly hold your pen or pencil above the paper, passively waiting for a thought to come. Focus for a few moments upon your heart before writing your answer. Write down whatever thoughts come into your mind, and then pause for more, without looking over what you have just written. Be like an impartial secretary taking down dictation. Force yourself to begin writing something, anything, even if it initially seems to come from your Intellect. Sometimes you will write down a few words without knowing what the next word is going to be, and at other times thoughts will come in clusters forcing you to write rapidly before you miss them. This is not the same as automatic writing. It often feels like these are your own thoughts that are coming to you. However, upon later reading, they might convey a simple wisdom that will impress you. At all times keep an open mind as if you are actually communicating with an attentive mentor and with the expectation that answers will come.

I was impressed by the ability of virtually every one of my patients to receive significant answers when directed gently and seriously to address their problems or questions to God. Each person had a preferred way of addressing God. Some felt more comfortable with "Higher Self," "Divine Being," "Inner Being," "Allah," "Divine Mother" or "Heavenly Father." My own preference is "Lord" or "Jesus." Young children often like to use the word "Angel," and are also surprisingly good at receiving answers.

After a hesitant start, the majority of subjects would soon begin picking up speed with their writing until they reached a point where they felt finished. Some began to produce intellectual answers in response to my prodding, but as they persisted in writing, almost all would begin to sense ideas coming from a different level. After reviewing their "answers" some would exclaim, "This is not something I would usually write." Others became emotional while they were writing and stated that the feelings were more meaningful than the words that came to them. Answers would consistently come that often led to the exploration of new possibilities that they had not explored before. Where did these ideas originate?

The universe is run by an unfathomable consciousness that we tend to take for granted. Something more than our conscious mind is also running our bodies. The simple act of digesting a mouthful of food and converting it into energy or into muscles or bone is a task so complex that the science of biochemistry is continually studying it and making new discoveries. Consider a woman who is pregnant. She has a few simple responsibilities in regard to taking care of her health, but she cannot fathom the miracle that is occurring within her. Can you even imagine the consciousness it requires to create a healthy baby! What if this same consciousness could be used to run your life? Wouldn't that be a comparatively much simpler task? And why shouldn't this resource be available to you?

Do not worry, before you begin, what you shall write, how you shall write or even for the purpose of obtaining a specific product. It involves a process that releases thoughts and emotions and reduces resistance to receiving answers from Higher sources. Because its real value is so non-specific, it is common to put it off until later, believing that you have so many other more important things to do. There must be a strong determination to persevere, preferably at a regular time such as early morning upon awakening or at bedtime. Do not pause to read what you are writing. This helps to take it out of the realm of an intellectual project.

When your pen reaches your paper, a thought or a few words may enter your mind. Continue questioning and force yourself to keep writing something, anything to keep the flow moving. Your brain acts like a keyboard receiving thoughts. Be like a stenographer taking dictation. All too often, it is our predetermined beliefs that stand in the way. When trying to reach

a higher level of intuition or inspiration, you ask the question
and then let the words flow without conscious thinking.

 Ideally, the communication is one of feeling/sensing that you
try to put into words. Once you start, you have taken the biggest
step. As with any creative project, it doesn't matter where you
start. It works by doing it. The answers are rarely specific actions
that you should take, but a new perspective, a shift in attitude,
or reassurance. Consider the idea that there is another way to
see life that can lead to expansion and that can bring to you any
experiences you desire.

Resistances to Communicating With God

What surprised me was that, despite a successful experience in
my comfortable office setting, very few subjects continued with
this exercise between our sessions. The usual excuse was "I
couldn't find the time." I would respond with the analogy that
we are all like astronauts, sent here by our Higher Selves to share
our earth experience. This leads to the question, "What if an
astronaut made a successful landing on Mars and, after the initial
excitement, all communication were lost for several days?
Everyone begins to frantically check their computers and to
manipulate the dials. Finally, Houston gets a voice signal,
'Harold here, everything A-okay.' The mission control captain
at Houston responds, "Harold, where have you been? We have
been worried sick about you." Harold replies, "Sorry, but I just

didn't have time to talk to you. There's so much to do here."
You might rightfully ask, "What could Harold be doing without
the guidance of Houston?" Similarly, what can anybody here
on earth do, that has any real significance, without the guidance
of their Higher Self?"

Of course, I was aware that "no time" was an excuse. It became
clear that my major problem would not be in convincing people
of the possibility of talking to God, but in overcoming the
resistances to talking to God.

Why is it so hard to listen to the voice that could save us from
needless worry and struggle? Most often, it is because it is
difficult to refute the voices in our childhood that told us we
were bad, wrong, guilty, lacking, not enough, unlovable,
rebellious, hateful, wrong, unworthy, too needy, or selfish in our
motives and intentions. There is also a common feeling of
unworthiness that must be overcome. How can we now believe
in that gentle voice that sees no wrong in us, understands our
loneliness and our pain, and that will persist in helping us despite
our doubts and fears? Our attitude toward God is not unlike
our attitude toward authority figures in general.

Freud discovered the universal phenomenon of resistance. In
fact, most of the interpretations made during psychoanalysis are
related to resistance. Resistance or stubbornness is probably one
of our greatest barriers to growth. It leads to a refusal to listen,

a refusal to change our mindset about life, a refusal to admit that we don't know, or that we're scared, or that we might have been mistaken.

Sometimes there are ways of getting around resistances without attacking them directly. Here is an example: One woman came to me with Chronic Fatigue Syndrome. I have found that chronic fatigue is often the result of closing down the emotional center in order to deny an intolerable life situation. She asked for help, and received the answer: *"We have been waiting for you. Do not be afraid of shedding your old skin to grow into a whole new life."*

Although the message was very brief and simple, she left my office encouraged and with a feeling of being loved, deeper than she had ever felt before. However, she called me that weekend to tell me that she had been suffering from a headache and nausea. These symptoms were accompanied by the feeling that her mother would no longer love her. She explained, "All of my thoughts were processed through her as I was growing up. Now I feel as if I am discounting her by turning elsewhere for strength." She had broken a silent contract with her mother that she had made as an infant, which was her mother's requirement to maintain a love bond. Until now, this contract with her mother had remained totally unconscious. We did an exercise using mental imagery to obtain her mother's permission, with the promise that she would ask God some questions on how she might be a more understanding daughter. Her internalized mother was glad to agree to this arrangement, and this dramatically alleviated her symptoms.

I soon collected a lengthy list of resistances to contacting God:

- *I don't feel deserving enough to write to God.*
- *I'm not sure that God is really listening.*
- *I'm not sure I will like the answers I get.*
- *I haven't any more room in my head for new information that might only add to my confusion.*
- *I think that I already know the answers, but I'm afraid to rock the boat, and I'm doing the best I can.*
- *I have enough people telling me what I should be doing.*
- *I'm not going to be able to follow His suggestions.*
- *I'm too tired and I don't have enough courage or self-discipline to change.*
- *Making a connection might reveal that this life really has no meaning and that everything I have clung to as being important has no meaning either.*
- *What could God possibly tell me to make a difference?*
- *God needs to prove Himself before I let Him into my head.*
- *Where was He when I needed Him?*
- *I'm tired of being told to be more considerate, kind, and loving to other people.*
- *I'm tired of being told that everything I'm doing is wrong.*
- *I'm too pissed!*

Following are some of the more important resistances that
deserve a thoughtful response:

What if I disagreed with God?

That's a necessary part of the process of your becoming a unique
being. God does not judge your sand castles, but He might
suggest that you build them a little farther from the waves. You
can always rebuild, so it doesn't really matter. You have an
infinite amount of sand and resources. You have an infinite
amount of chances. Rebellion is a necessary part of your
development. God supports you through all the experiences that
you think you need or want. He would like to break your cycle
of repeated bad experiences that you don't need anymore. It is
very difficult to break these cycles without His support.

*Is there anything you should not ask God? If I believe my
traditional church teachings, there are a whole lot of things in
life I shouldn't say in front of God. Just like I shouldn't say
them in church. I mean, God doesn't know about – or at least
approve of – sex; and stealing, and lying, and riding my bike on
Sunday, and a whole lot of other things. I'd never dare use
"bad" words in front of him, and – well, the list just goes on
and on.*

You can approach God with any emotion. In fact, the stronger
the emotion the more open is the door of communication. I have
often counseled parents who were upset by the fact that their

son or daughter came out with the words, "I hate you." Rather than holding this feeling inside, their child dared to show enough trust in the relationship to express it. This outburst should be seen as an attempt to establish a bond of love that seems temporarily broken. This statement comes from a projection of hurt in which that child felt invalidated or unloved or, perhaps, felt rejected in favor of another sibling. Once you know this you can answer in a number of ways such as, "Now what did I do to make you say that?" It becomes an opportunity to strengthen the bond. How much better that children express their angry feelings rather than nurse them and let them fester while seeking for reasons to justify them. That is how the ego works with private thoughts and why people who are relatively silent and isolated become more paranoid and depressed over   time.

How Private Thoughts Isolate Us

Frankly, my most difficult problems and the ones I don't like telling my best friend – or my therapist – or anyone can really be embarrassing. If I'm not doing the right things I'm told I won't get into Heaven—banished from His place. I'm caught between a rock and a hard place. So, what I tell God depends a lot on who or what I believe Him to be, and maybe on what I believe myself to be. Help! I think I need some new definitions.

You are being held captive by your private thoughts. Children tend to go inside and create a world composed of secret thoughts.

Private thoughts are filled with fears and grievances. Private thoughts are repetitive tapes that keep you stuck in the same situation with the same problems. Private thoughts obsessively focus upon your deficiencies, weaknesses, and limitations. They contribute to your feeling different, alone, or alienated. However, these negative private thoughts lose their power when brought to the light of day. Release all of your private thoughts by putting them down on paper, and then stop all judgment so that you can receive new thoughts. Thoughts that come from your Higher Mind are forgiving, creative, and uplifting.

When you try to find an identity by being busy, getting recognition from others, or trying to meet impossible goals, this is not only unrewarding and stressful but leads to a deeper state of unconsciousness and not to more self-awareness. You can only know who you are and what your true purpose is by remaining in constant communication with your Creator. You of yourself can do nothing. Everything depends upon getting in touch with the desires and needs of your true feelings and your willingness to allow God to help you. It does sound like this is asking for miracles. But that is how the truly important major events in your life really occur. If positive miracles do not appear often enough in your life it is because you have too low expectations of what you deserve. Growth can only come from the constant asking of new questions. And who can refuse the student who asks with openness and the full expectation of receiving an answer? Ask for help in changing your perceptions about the world and the nature of your problems. Redefining yourself is intimately related to changing your perceptions and impressions about the world.

So, let your daily dialogues be a clearing place for your private thoughts, all of which God knows anyway. Your link to God is as close as your link to your own mind. But your little mind has become separated from the greater Mind of Light and filled with private thoughts that keep you isolated and fearful of God, believing that He would punish you for your sins if He could read your mind. Quite the contrary is true. He would embrace you and comfort you for all the needless pain and suffering you have brought upon yourself.

God knows all about your anger and fear.
It comes from the feeling of separation.

God knows all about your negative state of mind.
It comes from the feeling of limitation of being trapped in a physical body.

God knows all about your anguish and despair.
It comes from the blocking off of creative energies, which makes your heart's deepest desires appear to be unreachable.

To all of your endless problems and questions there is really just one answer : the experience of connection that comes from no resistance.

Joanne's Resistance

When Joanne came to me she had extreme ambivalence toward her feelings and invited me to read about this in one of her journal entries:

> When I try to open myself up to feelings, I realize I really don't want to feel everything. I have carefully set up a system to keep me from doing just that. Why?
>
> I don't want to feel the loss of any more people I love when they die. I don't want to be tied to people who go up and down – pulling my feelings, my circumstances, my stable life into imbalance and disarray. I don't want to be put into pain and upset because I am connected to others, because every hurt, every stupid move, every big event that happens to them pulls and tugs at me and shifts my life. When I am connected to them I am shifted from my point of balance. I don't want others to affect me that way. I don't want to be dependent on them for my balance, or security, or happiness.
>
> Being *disconnected* from everyone leaves me lonely, without resources. Being *connected* to them leaves me vulnerable to every upset and hurt and difficult life situation that others move into.

So, I decided to be on my own. Then what? Life can hit me with blows that come directly to me. At least it's only my own stuff, not theirs. Illness, lack, limitations, frustration, separation - I try to anticipate all the possibilities in life, but can't always, so then I am broadsided by the unexpected. And I can't reach the part of me that might be of help. I'm supposed to be happy all the time in order to keep the door to inner connection open. I can't always do that because then I feel vulnerable to whatever comes.

I have a better intellectual understanding of connection to Inner Being than many, but I can't seem to get through and dissolve this barrier. So, what good am I to myself, let alone anyone else? If I can't connect inner guidance to outer life, what does it matter if there is an inner connection?

I can't stay partially numb (damn it!). I can't tolerate being completely unconscious. And I can't find a way to completely connect. That leaves me nowhere, and no way of finding me or making my life tolerable. I know a lot, but I can't make things work for me. This is the worst of all possible worlds. So, I don't want it!

Joanne felt trapped in a dilemma that had no solution until I introduced her to the steps of making a genuine connection to God. Her journal, then, rapidly took on a new direction, and one filled with enthusiasm.

Joanne's New Journal

All of my life I have longed and searched for a best friend, a helpmate, a supporter – someone who was always on my side, who would love me unconditionally. When I was first introduced to the concept of writing to God with the purpose of having a real connection with the ultimate source of unconditional love and power, it was a dream come true. At the same time I was very afraid that I would fail. Because my life had been devoid of the real connections I so deeply desired, I held negative belief systems about my self-worth and my value to others – God included. My bottom line greatest fear was that I was empty and not real and there was nothing to connect with. I also felt that there must be something lacking in me and I wouldn't be able to catch on because of performance anxiety. Another issue was, "Would God find me worthy of an answer?" "Did He care about me?" "Could I trust Him or His answers?"

My desire for connection overpowered my fears and so I was willing to take the risk. I was encouraged to sit quietly, breathe and go into a meditative state allowing my skeptical mind to melt away. I wasn't even sure what to ask. I didn't want God to think I was silly or immature, as if I could hide from God. It gradually became almost like a dialogue with a friend. I usually start by describing my feelings and then arrive at a question. I can immediately tell when I am connecting by the feeling in my heart – a subtle expansion or contraction of my energy. I can now easily move myself back and wait for the answers.

Waiting can be the hardest part, but now the answers seem to flow quite easily.

This kind of communication seems different than other kinds of writing that I have done. The answers seem to come from a deep and wise place of knowing. I totally trust the answers. They definitely see the bigger picture and they have given me tremendous insight and compassion for others and myself. There are so many benefits from this relationship. Of primary importance is the feeling of connection that I feel to a secret source of love, support and power. It colors everything and is allowing me to feel safe and more open to the natural flow of love and joy. It is a continual reflection of my relationship to existence. I am learning about co-creation, surrender and trust. I have found God to be a great partner and a very patient one. Here are some of the answers that I received:

Q. *I grew up in a household where there was hardly enough food to eat. I always felt a lack of what the other kids had. I still feel as if I can barely hold things together. How can I stop worrying about money?*

A. Lack does not exist in the universe. It is possible, from the physical perspective, to experience the phenomenon of lack in the same sense that darkness is a phenomenon. Light is a reality, as is energy flow. The absence of anything is an imagined phenomenon. It is not possible for ultimate reality to extend lack. Lack is not a substance that can be extended. Therefore, the only substance, the only manifestation, that can be extended, is abundant manifestation of all that is desired, all that is needed, and all that serves purpose within this dimension. Fear of not having is registered as a request. There are no limits because this is a world of imagination. Take yourself to a place for a special treat for yourself. Take some blank paper with you and write down some of your beliefs about lack. You might discover areas of yourself that you were minimally aware of until now.

Q. I always felt that nothing I started would come to completion.

A. Yes. But remember, it is your energy that allows or blocks this. Are you able to begin to change your belief system around this? In childhood your basic energies were held in by "Do Not Open" doors. There is another way to see life that can lead to expansion. If a being wishes to open any door to any area of life, the beginning step is always quieting the thinking area rather than the obverse, which you were taught. The thinking mechanism is only a conduit through which many energies pass. The shift to a higher energy involves a new paradigm and can be done with a spirit of discovery. Barriers are like columns of dark energy, and can be somewhat intimidating. But when seen closely from a calm level they begin to dissolve.

Q. I feel as if I have wasted so much of my life that it is too late to make any major changes now.

A. Rather than blame yourself for what you would see as unused or empty intervening years, just know that the seed was planted when it could be planted, knowing that it would come to growth and fruition later. And so the invitation is as fresh today as it was in the past. As in golf, the ball needs to be played where it lies. One cannot replay earlier strokes. The stroke you make now changes everything including the significance of the previous stroke. The earth dimension is intended to be one of exploration and creation. Questions are formed which compel answers that in turn move us into new directions. Because of its various input of sensations on physical and emotional levels, there may be confusion. But the intent is to give pleasure. If one becomes as a child again and makes fresh conclusions, new perceptions begin to dominate the life experience.

Q. I am afraid of wanting anything because of the disappointment of not getting it.

A. Want is a launching pad to enormous benefit. Closed doors are not locked doors. Shift your energy from despair to anticipation. The energy of frustration or discouragement can become the energy that overcomes the inertia to launch oneself into a new area. It is when the opportunity for positive change is greatest.

Q. I am worried about my husband who is not taking care of his health.

A. When one close to you is involved in a serious illness there often is a sense of urgency to move out and help; however, each energy system already has within itself the resources to fill its own needs. Extending our caring to another is always blessed, but never with the assumption of the other person's powerlessness to help himself. Know, as in poker, when to hold and when to fold. Taking on the agony of another never lightens their burden. The interjection of joy, confidence, and peace is what will act as a balm to the afflicted one. Ask yourself, "Who am I outside of this relationship?" Out of "Who am I" the proper action will come. Those who judge you will be like far distant echoes. Firmly and lovingly offer alternative resources. Do not accept full responsibility for his seeking for help. There is always the danger of loss of self in a relationship with too much interdependency.

Q. How can I more fully experience my Higher Self?

A. The Higher Self seeks to reach the earth self. Open a pathway by sitting near a tree. Feel the sensations in the belly, and with your hands on your belly, focus on the sensation and let it spread though your body. Become accustomed to feeling good with no associations, no words, and no language. From this base, yearn for Divine Mother love. Comfort will come from the opening made by the intensity of the yearning. Make affirmations: "I have every right to experience a state of comfortableness and self-acceptance. Among the areas of energy of earth beings is a cord or connection uniting every level of consciousness to the Inner Self that has all knowledge available to it.

Gloria's Experience of Resistance

Connecting to God through writing is a wonderful technique to uncover answers to my problems. I found the results of writing in this way unbelievable. I connected with it instantly while learning the process in my therapist's office, and I felt that I was truly connecting to a different place within myself, a place of greater wisdom. I had no idea what I was writing, and when I read it back I couldn't believe I actually wrote it. I never imagined that I could have thought the answers that I read. I was excited to try it at home, and finally have the day-to-day answers I needed. Whenever I try to discuss my problems with my friends or family I always seem to get nowhere. People want to help but they usually only have instant shallow answers that just makes me feel more confused.

That night, while waiting to go to sleep, I felt excited about how wonderful it would be to do the writing on my own. The next day I had all sorts of things I needed to do: the dishes, the laundry, and picking up around the house. I had to get my daughter off to school and give my son his breakfast as well as my own breakfast. I kept thinking about the writing every so often and knew I would have plenty of time to write while my son took his nap in the afternoon. Soon after he began his nap, the telephone rang. I took care of the important business call and the paperwork that followed the call. I also made a few needed phone calls, and before you know it my son was awake and I had to leave to pick up my daughter from school. After bustling about with the kids later in the day, I looked forward to relaxing and going through the mail while watching a little television. When my husband came home we went through each other's day while dinner came and went and I soon found myself relaxing into my favorite television show. The day was gone.

Lying in bed, I felt disappointed that I didn't do the writing that I wanted so very much to do. I promised myself I would definitely get to it tomorrow. Days passed and I still hadn't found the time to do any writing. It seemed everything else was taking priority. One day I actually sat down at the computer with great intention, but found myself caught up in a game of solitaire. I really wanted to win just once before starting to write. But by the time that was accomplished, I had a headache and another day passed without writing to God.

By the time I met with my therapist again I had found a few desperate moments to write to God. It seemed to help, but I didn't feel the deep sense of connection that I had the first time. My therapist asked me if I had been doing the writing and I sheepishly told him that I had done a little bit, but that it was hard to find the time. He looked at me and chuckled and began telling me a story about others who had the same excuse. "They just couldn't find the time to talk to God.", he said. "But you did find the time to come to see me, so I guess I should be flattered." At that moment a light went off in my head and I realized I had been doing just that. I hadn't had time to talk to God! What kind of a crazy thing is that to say? I was allowing everything else to take priority over God. I was shocked at what I was doing. After all, this was important to me. I truly wanted to find the answers and to become a happy, contented person, to become my ideal woman, and to be at peace with the world and with myself. I realized I had put all these other things in front of God, my direct source to all that I wanted.

As I left my therapist's office, I was once again energized and excited about writing to God, and saddened that I hadn't been connecting all this time. Again days went by, but this time I closely observed and watched the excuses and how I kept putting the writing aside. Some excuses, I must submit, were valid and others just plain resistance. I was witnessing a real struggle within myself. I could feel the tug-of-war and the great resistance to doing it for myself. I noticed all the fears I had, and when I couldn't stand the struggle any longer, I finally forced myself to sit down and write out the fears. As long as the fears were in the way I couldn't get to the real answers that I so very much needed. I uncovered more fears than I ever thought I had. "What if I don't get the right answers?" "What if the answers I get are not real?" "What if it doesn't work by myself?" I even had the fear, "What if it works?" I realized how most of my fears sounded ridiculous even though my feelings of them were so overwhelming. I tackled these fears one by one and answered most of them with, "So what?" Anything would be better than being stuck in fear and resisting God. As I wrote it all down, I could see it all so much more clearly than trying to just think it all out in my head. I was able to dissipate the fears and by doing so I felt so much more relaxed and centered within myself. I was now ready to connect with God, even though I think I had already been doing it by sharing my fears.

I wrote down a question, closed my eyes, and took a few deep breaths while imagining a white light coming from the highest point in the universe and flowing straight through the top of my head into my heart, through my arm, to my hand, and out through my pen. I imagined this all with as much detail as I could, and then I began to write the answer to my question without thinking at all. I just let my hand float across the paper. I wrote and wrote, barely knowing what the words were saying and, yet, having a great sense of a connection to the Source. It felt right, it felt good, and I wrote until I felt a sense that it was time to stop. When I finished I glanced up at the clock. What I thought was just a few minutes had been nearly an hour. I looked down at the paper where there were several pages of words, and I couldn't believe I had written so much. As a read them I couldn't believe it was really me who wrote this. The answers were amazingly just what I needed to hear, although I never would have known it on my own. There is no way I could have thought of this on my own.

At one point while I was writing I got a bit frightened because I felt like I was nearly out of my body or somehow not attached to my hand. My hand was moving but I wasn't thinking about it. It was almost like my hand was only being used to do the writing. I could stop it anytime if I decided to, but as long as I just focused on the light coming through me and relaxed with it, the writing just naturally and easily floated out of me like a steady flowing river of knowledge. I was so excited and felt so exhilarated by the entire experience. I felt centered and focused the rest of the day and I found I was in much better spirits than I usually am. I was much more tolerant with my family and had a general contentment about me. I was able to do the writing a few more times that week and I was getting great results. It felt like I had my own therapy session going on with myself and getting the answers that were really hitting me at a place that felt right.

Soon things began coming up again, I had some company from out of town and my routine was interrupted and so the writings got pushed to the side again. It was like a bad habit coming back to haunt me, almost like I was revisiting where I had been before. Only this time I knew what to do and remembered how it had worked before. The resistances are powerful and plenty but it's no different than any of the bad habits you need to kick. I saw the world around me and realized how many people I see every day that have a chance to truly feel good and they don't do anything but stay stuck where they are. I saw how we all get stuck in beating ourselves up, and when we do get an answer that is real and life-changing, we just sort of shrug it off and figure it can't be that easy. "If it's too easy it must not be real," we say to ourselves. And yet when we know something to be real in our gut and our heart, no one on earth can change our belief that it is real. "So why do we doubt?" I asked myself. Is it just a bad habit to willfully overcome? Do I just want to be unhappy because it feels so much more familiar? Or, maybe it would be too hard to live in true happiness and love for myself. After all, if I cared, then there's a lot more to lose.

I am still struggling with the writing, but I am doing it on a more regular basis. I finally decided that if I keep it up I would eventually form new habits that make me feel good instead of bad. And I would much rather live the rest of my life in a better state of mind than to live it as I have so far.

Overcoming The Fear of Love

I have found that the basic core of all resistances can be traced to a defense against love – both the receiving and the wanting of it. I once believed that children were most crippled by the lack of genuine parental caring and love. I have since found that even more crippling is their expression of love that is not returned, and especially when it raises the reaction of withdrawal. The innocent love of a child is more than many parents feel worthy of receiving and returning. The fear of love must be discussed if we want to understand and to receive God's love for us.

In all of our strivings, all we ever really want is love. But we have not been taught how to receive love unconditionally, and so, inwardly, we feel unworthy of it and cannot accept it even when it is offered unless we feel that we have earned it. This, then, is the sad paradox of man. Without a secure, loving sense of self, we defensively hurt those closest to us by shutting them off. Without self-love we are unable to receive the only thing that really matters. Yet we are driven to strive endlessly in search of it. The resistance we have to God, Who represents the highest form of love, can be understood in terms of our misperception about the love that we have experienced since birth, which was primarily conditional love. Children in our present social milieu are taught prejudice, competition, comparison, judgment, and conditional love that must be earned through achievement. Children lose their sense of uniqueness and become selfish in the pursuit of trying to become "special" by earning conditional love. This is invariably where all of our "problems" begin.

All children suffer some form of invalidation of their inner feelings and of their worth. By the time they become an adult, a sense of unworthiness is already fixed in their mind as a "given." That is why people are afraid to look within and, instead, project their self-judgments onto others. You can learn a lot about yourself by noticing how you criticize other people.

You believe that love hurts because, with rare exceptions, the radiant love you projected outward as an infant was not returned with the same energy. You interpreted this as a rejection of who you were. Therefore you now believe that an important relationship cannot last. Your fear and confusion about love is what keeps it from coming to you.

Most people are terrified of feelings. From the time you first experienced the anguish of invalidation, you built a wall of invulnerability around yourself. Your emotions work very much like your immune system. You are afraid to be hurt again, and each time you believe that you have been rejected the pain is stronger. As an infant, your emotional center resonated to the pain of your parents and you believed that most feelings involved pain. But pain is not feeling. The primary cause of pain is the resistance to feelings. The ego is a mechanism of defense based upon fear and the belief that you are separate and vulnerable in a competitive and uncaring world. The ego does not believe in unconditional love. To love someone is to give them power over you. The ego contaminates love with fear and puts a price tag on it as well. How do you ask for love in a world where giving is seen as a burden? If you complain, you are attacked. If you are needy, others withdraw from you. You are afraid of love because love is always open to doubt and can be quickly withdrawn. The ego creates God in its own image, and who would want to bond with that tyrant who is filled with judgment and who makes impossible demands upon us?

Your belief structures are the bricks that become the building blocks of your reality. These feelings and beliefs begin from the time you are in your mother's womb. Your parents give to you the lenses that you view your world through as you grow into adulthood. Everyone, to some extent, believes that they are unworthy of love unless they earn it. Some even feel unworthy to live. You can tell by the shallow way in which they breathe. You can tell by their inability to play and to laugh. You can tell by the way in which they judge the unworthiness of other people.

All people suffer the grief of separation that is experienced as loneliness. Some try to fill their loneliness by being constantly busy while others try to fill their yearning to be whole by finding a partner who, himself or herself, is not whole. The greatest power in the universe is love, and what you truly are as a living Soul is a vibrational frequency of a loving thought by God that is given life through emotion. When you know the immense love contained within your own Inner Core you can create your own reality. Until you accept and truly love every facet of who you are, you do not know what love is.

Love is the vibration of the creative force of God. It is the expression of God indistinct from the Essence of God. It is the life force without which nothing can exist. On the higher levels it is experienced as both light and sound—the Light of God and the Word of God. When a finger of the Soul descends into matter there is a downgrading of vibration as well as a splitting into polarities of this energy, the better to examine and to understand it. White light passing through a quartz crystal breaks up into many colors allowing us to see the possiblity of creating beautiful paintings that would be impossible with white light alone. Look at the possibilities of infinite interactions that would not be possible if we did not have the polarity of yin and yang.

When consciousness enters a physical body we become disconnected from our Soul by the attractions of the five senses and the vulnerability of the physical body that leads us to close off our emotions, which are the language of the Soul, and to seek unconsciousness because of fear. Relying solely upon our surface Intellect is like going into a deep sleep because we become unconscious of the invisible forces beyond our five senses and, regardless of how active we become or how productive our dreams seem to be, we are really sleepwalking. When we wake up, usually at the time of death, we can take nothing with us other than what we learned in our dream. Unless we know we are asleep we cannot awaken while still in a physical body. Yet this is our purpose, namely despite the illusion of feeling unimportant or "nothingness", to follow the urgings of our Soul to slowly discover our birthright as a child of God.

Every action that is not loving, hence selfish, regardless of the monetary reward that appears to justify it, makes us uncomfortable and defensive on some level. This is the basis for what has been called the "neurotic conflict," the disparity between the actions of our personality not in harmony with our Soul. The personality is tied to the world. But there is nothing to win or to lose here. We are fighting against the shadows of our own projections. Only love will dissolve the shadows and free us. We must make our world beautiful before we can leave it to move to a higher level of existence. You do not need to search for love. You only have to ask with intent and desire for the experience of unconditional love. It is all around you, awaiting your reception of it.

Reasons For Maintaining A Daily Dialogue With God

Your daily dialogue with God is a chronicle of new feelings and understandings that come as the result of observing and living your life with more awareness. It can help to bring all of your secret fears to light where your rational Intellect can more easily handle them. It records your personal process of removing barriers and interfacing more intimately with life. Then solutions will come with fresh questions as you train yourself to listen. It is something like establishing a telepathic communication with your Creator and understanding that His purpose for you is much better than that which you, in your state of confusion, are now trying to decide for yourself. This kind of observing and listening helps you to realize that you are far more important than the little physical speck you call a body. This is the simplest and clearest way to observe that your life has a pattern with a meaningful direction and purpose.

There are many occasions when your mind is troubled by a flood of confusing thoughts. You want to make the right decisions, but it is difficult for you to know what to do. If you are like most people, your belly is often filled with fear or else tight with anger at the insecure place you hold in the world. Your brain is tired of thinking. There is a sense of lack, coupled with self-recrimination, so that peace cannot be found either inside or outside of yourself. Your time has been heavily mortgaged, so there is little time left for play. You may feel simultaneously restless, lazy, overwhelmed, bored, and "on your own." Life, at times seems so difficult that you feel like saying, "I quit," but you don't know how to quit.   You seek advice and everyone tells you something different or something that doesn't work. Nobody seems to know where they are going or what they are doing. But everyone seems to be very busy, and there is not much time to do the necessary things beyond basic survival.

Instead of closing off and trying to ignore the things you're worried about, acknowledge them fully and, at the same time, acknowledge your not knowing what you can do about them. Sometimes you have an initial impulse to do something, maybe even an excitement about it. But, quickly it becomes overridden by the feeling of overwhelm. This is accompanied by disparaging thoughts such as: "I can't do it." "I don't know how." "I don't have time." "I'll be wasting my time." "I have too many other things to do."   Have you noticed that the people who are the most frenetically busy all the time, have very little of substance to show for it? Refuse to rehearse to yourself your grievances against the world. Shift your mind from sulking and bitterness to an openness of how God can use you to improve your environment and, with this, the wellbeing of everyone around you. God knows. God understands. God has answers – for *you*. Wouldn't it be worth a bit of your time each day to ask your questions and to practice receiving answers that could change your life? It is surprising how many people believe that this might work for others but not for themselves.

It doesn't matter whether or not you feel unworthy.   When you suffer from emotional pain or feelings of lack or helplessness, this can be used positively to motivate you to turn to a higher Source for the energy and strength you need. The attitudes and the behavior of the people in your present environment are not a barrier although, admittedly, it is difficult to grow without the encouragement of friends who are also interested in personal growth. However, you will gradually draw like-minded people to you as you progress. Remember, you are on a very personal and very important journey. As you awaken you will initially feel sad when you become aware of how asleep most other people really are.

When writing to God, it is perfectly acceptable to hold, for a time, onto the resistance of doubt in order to temper the fixed patterns within your consciousness that are afraid of change. Do not hesitate because you feel unworthy. The more fear, guilt, hatred, and self-disgust you have, the more necessary and valuable it is for you to ask for help. And do not be discouraged by your weaknesses, failures, and behaviors of the past. These were all necessary to develop your own uniqueness, strength of character, and humility to open up to God. Because you cannot see the whole picture, you cannot be a judge of your own progress. Some of your greatest advances you have judged as failures and some of your steps backward you have evaluated as success.

There is always the fear that we cannot do what is expected of us to do to make a significant change in our lives. And what if the process of trying to reach God fails? That would be the ultimate rejection. It's safer to call it "stupid," or a "waste of time." And, perhaps, at first, your doubt is so strong that you have difficulty receiving an answer. It also could mean that the answer is being blocked by your expectation of something different than you need to hear.   Do not see this as a rejection but your own resistance to listening. Many of your questions might not be answered in the manner that you expect. If you have already made an angry decision about someone, your emotions may over-ride your intuition and, instead, give you an answer to justify your suspicions. God will not make judgments about other people, but may gently guide you into trusting your own innate sensitivity and ability to attune to the moral character or intentions of others. Instead of asking whether your husband or wife is faithful to you or if your son is taking drugs, ask how you might strengthen your relationship with your spouse or how you can support your son over a difficult period in his life.

Sometimes when obstacles seem insurmountable, a person may pray for help in overcoming them without realizing that he is stubbornly persisting to struggle against his own best interests. Many of us have intentions and good ideas that we want God to support. But this may not be God's agenda, and He is not likely to support the ego that is trying to lead you in the wrong direction. For example, Joanne prayed for several years to be of more assistance in helping her husband's glass business to succeed when this was not the intended direction he was meant to go. Yet, he persisted until he had a serious physical breakdown and had to be placed on disability. One year later the ideal work situation opened up to him that he had been too fearful to look for before. (see <u>Jim on Mindset</u> page 165)

One woman challenged God with: *"How can you expect me to believe in You when all during my childhood I prayed to make my parents stop fighting, and nothing ever happened to change things?"* The response she received surprised her: "You were asking Me to do something that I could not do inasmuch as I have given all My children free will. You were watching the result of your parents making wrong choices so that you can make better choices in your own life."

Young children can gain significant consolation from any adult who explains to them that their parents' problems are not their fault. If both of her parents had acknowledged their problem and prayed for help, then positive change would very likely have occurred. It is interesting that, despite this woman's upset with her parents, she tended to reproduce her childhood environment of controversy and conflict in her present home. It was a pattern that was handed down from generation to generation. When she saw this, she was able to forgive her parents and herself as well. She stated firmly, "It ends here!" Awareness, with a genuine asking for help to break her addiction to her parents' behavior, gradually brought about the positive changes she had come to me to help her to make.

During childhood you experience many things over which you have little or no control. These experiences force you to ask questions around a theme that is related to your life purpose. As an adult, you will have opportunities to resolve these emotional issues and to move to a higher level of personal power.

Your very act of asking with feeling and your willingness to be helped raises your vibration to a new level and, with it, your whole environment as well. Your mind, your perceptions, and your Intellect are filled with the reality of this material world. And because your real Self is not of this world, you must try to put all previous learning behind you and to listen with the ears of a newborn child. You need only to be still, to empty your head of the busy clutter of the day, leaving God's voice a place to enter. At first faintly, and then ever more clearly His Presence will become a reality to you. You will never be asked to do anything that you do not truly wish to do. You will never be told to do something that you cannot do. You will not lose any part of yourself that you are not already trying so hard to discard. It is a way to claim your birthright as a child of God.

> Approach God, the I Am, with love, or even with anger, but never with a sense of intimidation.

> Approach God with the awe and innocence of a child.

> Approach God with an open heart, awaiting good news. Because that is what the Truth has to offer.

Approach God with a humble Intellect, trying its best to record the experience, but realizing that it can never fully comprehend it.

Ask directly for what you really want:
> A feeling of being connected,
>
> A feeling of protection,
>
> An increase of love in your life,
>
> A sense of happiness, satisfaction, and purpose.

My Own Initial Experience of Writing to God

I have been keeping a journal of writing to God on an almost daily basis for the past thirty years. It has definitely helped me to temper my moods, to see things in a more positive light, and to pass through periods of disappointment and frustration. During this time I have learned more about this process and how it works to gradually detect patterns of thinking and behavior that must be continually changed and upgraded. I would like to share my very first attempt to talk to God in September of 1970, when I was just beginning to learn about meditation. It has been a very personal thing until now. I addressed God as "Lord," my inner teacher.

Q. Lord, why am I not more aware?

A. You are only as aware as you dare to be. All that you wish to be, you already are! You (and all others) have but to seize upon the special faculties which God has given to you, just as He has given you arms and hands that you may use for your enjoyment and creativity.

Q. But when I try to use them, something stops me. I think that I am afraid of failure.

A. Then you will surely fail! Nothing fails more than self-negation. But, more commonly, as in your case, there is a strong fear of success.

Q. Why should I be afraid of success? Why am I afraid of becoming more aware, or of developing psychic powers?

A. When the centers of the body are not at one with themselves, and there is much warring among the various members, then attempts at peace are made by disarming all concerned.

Q. But how can I be more at one with myself?

A. Desire it, ask for it, and be willing to receive, knowing that it is God's will that all men be omniscient so as to share more fully in His glory. Earthly parents cannot very often withstand the scrutiny of their children, whereas the Father in Heaven loves it.

Q. But apparently we are here (on earth) because this was misused. How can I be sure that I do not misuse whatever intelligence or power I have now?

A. Only this, that you keep constantly in mind the Source of all power, all force, and all intelligence, or else it will not be replenished.

Q. Lord, I would like to continue on and on asking questions, but feel I must stop now as if I have a limited quota. Is this true?

A. God wills that humans know all things. And He rejoices in answering all questions and filling all needs so long as this is asked of Him with true desire and in the spirit of love. God is never depleted. God never tires. God never becomes impatient – but men do.

I didn't appreciate the answers until rereading them weeks or even months afterward. In fact, I think that I tended to downplay the answers because I was afraid to believe that I was actually reaching a source as important as God. It was only much later that I realized that I had made a significant step in a direction that was to provide me with considerable support over the years. The biggest resistance I initially had against continually utilizing this resource was my inability to appreciate the unfathomable consciousness of God. God is acutely aware of our every thought and entire circumstances at every moment in time and is continually setting up situations to make us more aware of our motives and thinking patterns so that we can make the right choices. If we become angry at any time, it means that we have missed that particular opportunity for learning, by allowing fear to enter our heads.

Consider that every one of the trillion or more cells in each human body is like an entire universe of its own and that God is constantly aware of the activity of every one of them. In fact, God is aware of each atom in the universe and also the possibility and potentialities of its merging with every other atom in the universe at any given moment in time. That is far beyond our physiological brain's capacity to fathom.

A television set is just a big, useless box until that tiny needle from the cable is inserted in the back. Then it becomes alive with dozens of channels in full color from all over the world. Similarly, there may be no discernible difference between a man who is sleeping and a man who is dead. But one has the life force in him while the life force has been withdrawn from the other. God is the life force, like electricity, that energizes the movement and consciousness of every manifest thing.

I must share that while I am deeply
contemplating the meaning of the
preceding paragraphs I suddenly feel

*God's presence fill the space all
around me. I am awed by His
unfathomable omnipresence. How
can He be here so focused and aware
of every object, book and page in
every book on my bookshelves and still
be everywhere else in the universe!*

Mother earth offers herself as a platform for our Soul to project
a small portion of itself to experience an infinite variety of
growth experiences in physical form. By limiting the mind to
the five senses, and sequencing events through the use of time,
it enables us to join God in the evolution of our own
consciousness.

This can be a time for Soul searching that need not be painful,
but more like a releasing and healing. The innate fear of looking
at your doubts and insecurities, what you believe are your
weaknesses and the disowned parts of your personality that are
angry and hurting, are very strong. But once you succeed in
bringing all of this to awareness with a feeling of acceptance,
there will likely be a sigh of relief. Our denials are what keep
us in a constant state of inner conflict. These denials consist of
all of the things we believe we cannot do, the things we are afraid
to face about ourselves, that we think we cannot change, and
our blindness to the amount of love that is constantly supporting
us.

For People Who Are Too Busy

One of my patients persisted in asking about the availability of this higher support and the importance of putting it into practice on a regular basis:

Q. God, what should people write about? Should they do it every day? What if they say that they are too busy?

A. They should write about anything or everything; even the smallest event has meaning. Even a small event is an event and a vehicle for learning. Yes, it would be good to write something every day to keep a connection, but one should not feel pressured to do so. It is like a conversation with one's loved one. Do you call your closest friends because you want to or because they insist that you do? Whatever is genuine is the best. Again, they should write what is foremost in their minds. Nothing is too trivial.

If they are too busy, that is sad for them. They were not meant to be so busy. It interferes with their learning. It is akin to a hamster running a wheel from compulsion, thoughtlessly running because that is the state one is in, not because one has chosen it. You all must learn that you can step off the wheel. There is no loss, even if ostensibly it appears to be seen as a failure. That having been said, the wheel, the running of it, is sometimes a necessary functional choice for the time and place.

If they are too busy, they are not ready. It is not the right moment. Not all are are willing to write, and you must accept that. It takes a threshold level of seriousness, the awareness that one can choose to make the choice to step off of the wheel. Fortunately, this trend is spreading. People are becoming tired of the running. More and more people are wishing to get off, not yet realizing that it is a simple choice, one step and one is off. Once this is clear, the process will be short and enlightening for these people, and it will spread further.

People are unaware of the ways that help is available to them to lighten their moods and to overcome the problems of the day. People do not realize the use to which their consciousness can be put. Just because they are unable to move a table or a chair by directing their thoughts, does not mean that they cannot alter their entire environment by raising the vibratory level of their thoughts. Those who are always flustered and in stress can never find rest by working harder. The tasks God gives are simple and few, and always for the purpose of joyful creative expression. The tasks that the ego gives are always impossible to complete. You cannot serve two masters. Those who serve the ego have no time to listen to God.

Perhaps you have already noticed that whenever you seriously decided to engage in any new activity to make a significant change in your life, whether it is an exercise program or a special diet to lose weight, there were always resistances against continuing. Old habits are very hard to break and most people do not have the will power to persist until they experience the desired changes that then can become self-reinforcing.

There is an old Japanese adage that gives these three basic instructions to insure success:

1. It must be very simple.
2. It must be done very repetitively.
3. It must be done with a sense of positive expectancy.

3

Ways in Which God Can Help

Let us consider the ways in which God can help to bring positive changes both to our sense of well being and to our immediate environment. God is the life force that flows through our bodies, giving us vitality and perfect health. However, our thinking mechanism puts up various resistances due to our fears and negative thinking patterns that results in low energy, disease, and aging. Our initial requests should be for help to clear our minds from out habitual negative thinking patterns. We literally live in our heads, and any Light we allow to enter in will bring with it a sense of peace.

Decisions we made in early childhood are often difficult or impossible to reverse later in life because of the emotional content holding them in place. It isn't so much what happened to you in childhood, but what you told yourself about it during, or shortly afterward, that creates the emotional charge that can remain with you for a lifetime. Many of these emotional links cannot be unhooked without a higher level of assistance.

I am reminded of a friend of mine in college. Bob was an engineering major, and upon graduation in the late 1950's he was approached with an enticing job offer to be part of a young crew that would inspect the large radar sites that were being built in Greenland. He was very conscientious on the job, and was able to note a number of significant omissions that he pointed out to his supervisor. Among other things, many reinforcing struts were omitted and the soldering of joints was four feet apart instead of the mandated two feet. His instructor was not appreciative of his findings, stating, "Listen, kid, you're being paid well. Just keep your mouth shut." He was persistent and confronted the foreman on the job. A few days later he asked if the work had been done to specifications, and got the response that everything was satisfactory. He stated that he was going up to the top to begin inspecting the structure. The foreman warned, "I wouldn't go up there if I were you, kid."

It was freezing weather. Nevertheless, Bob climbed up the large metal structure and, as he approached the top, his feet suddenly slipped out from under him because the metal had been heavily greased. His hands reached out wildly as he fell. One hand managed to luckily grip a horizontal strut. His body swung in space, held up by a tight grip on the metal strut, the only thing that was keeping him from falling some 60 feet down onto the cold concrete below. He gradually managed to bring his feet onto a metal crossbar and then attempted to release his hand so that he could climb down. However, his fingers would not let go. They had received such an emotional command to hold on, that the only way that he could release them was to take a screwdriver and to straighten each of them free from the bar one by one.

I see this incident as analogous to how emotionally charged premises are strongly held in place during early childhood and descend into the subconscious mind from where they influence all future perceptions and decisions. We do not have the power to overcome our negative, addictive thinking patterns without help. We need help in separating the "wheat from the tares," the positive and joyful thoughts from the thoughts that lead to depression and physical illness. We must literally ask the Holy Spirit to enter our heads and replace the thoughts that arise from unwanted past memories with thoughts of optimism, appreciation and peace. Just "working on them" doesn't work, and obsessing about them gives them added strength.

We are here for an important life experience, the significance of which is beyond our present comprehension. The life experience need not be unpleasant if we surrender our desperate struggles and hand over to God our tiresome burdens. God runs everything in the universe and we do not need to struggle "by the sweat of our brows" to accomplish the seemingly endless tasks that we try to accomplish alone by our free will. All mind is one. When our mind is consciously focused upon God, we are uplifted with inspiration and creativity. New opportunities begin to appear like miracles.

Putting Yourself In God's Place
In Answering Your Questions

One important thing that every person has to learn if they want to help people who come to them with a problem, is that merely understanding the problem or having an answer to it is not enough. The real task is to find a way to communicate a solution that would be understood, accepted and useful. People can only understand new ideas in small increments at a time. Thus, the answers you receive might seem too simple at first.

The following visual exercise or "mindtrip" should give you some idea of how limited we all are in accepting or comprehending any advise that goes more than a small step beyond our present level of understanding:

> **See yourself at a time when you were approximately half your present age. Think not only of the year, but visualize specifically where you were and what you were doing at that time. The mind thinks only in pictures. Pick a relatively neutral scene and ask yourself some questions about the person you see that you were then:**

> **Is this person self-aware? Does this person have a clear idea of the future and where he or she is headed? Is this person able to relate to others openly? Is this**

person prepared to deal effectively with the challenges that are coming up in the next couple of years? Does this person really know what a good relationship is all about? Is this person content, happy, and taking full advantage of all of the options that are available to make life more enjoyable?

After asking yourself a number of questions along these lines, then consider your present self and whether you could be a helpful mentor to that person if you could transport yourself into the past. What have you learned that would be helpful to that person you were and how would you be able to communicate it in a way that would be heard and accepted sufficiently to be put into practice? Can you see that what you have to offer would ideally have to be given in small doses because of that person's level of understanding, self-image, and mindset? Perhaps your biggest help would be in suggesting the proper questions that should be asked.

I recommend the above exercise for a number of reasons. It helps you to see that you have grown in many ways over the years just through the process of living. *You might also see that what you have learned of real value has come not so much from your greatest successes but what you may have considered, at the time, to be your biggest failures.* Therefore, count the gains you have made in your personal growth that might not have come to you in any other way, rather than review your past with regret.

The more you have learned, the more likely you are to now look back at the past and to decide that you could have done some things quite differently. *However, you cannot judge what is "good" or "bad" in your experiences unless viewed from a higher level.* Your growth can now proceed exponentially through your continual questioning.

Many of us have good intentions and good ideas that we want God to support. But God is not likely to support the ego that would lead you in the wrong direction. We all want to feel significant and we try to feel significant by being busy. But the inner work is the only real significant work that matters. There is a constant conflict between our loving inner Core and the attitudes of our ego that have a physiologic presence in your muscles and in the organs of your body. Left to our own devices we will continually stumble and make the wrong decisions. It is proper to put as much intrinsic value upon other people as upon ourselves. However, our ultimate intent is a closer fellowship to God and not the pleasing of ourselves or becoming obsessed with the pleasing of others. We are an affluent society dying from spiritual malnutrition.

You need to extend from a real center, one that will not be upended by whether another person likes it or not. Complaining is your greatest confession of not knowing who you are and not taking responsibility for your power. Once you feel guilty, your capability for normal functioning is damaged. Focus upon the energy you are now extending out to the world and to others.

Your task is not to seek for love, but to find all of the barriers within yourself that you have built up against love.

Suicidal Thoughts Are Not Uncommon

It is surprising how many of the general population, when seriously questioned, will admit to having had mild to moderate thoughts of suicide at more than one or more times in their life. These are almost always associated with feelings of helplessness or hopelessness. Statistics show that about 30,000 people commit suicide each year in the United States. Undoubtedly, many more commit suicide through careless "accidents," often with the help of alcohol or drugs. But an even far greater number of suicides are committed each year by heart attacks and cancer that can be the subconscious mind's way of escaping an intolerable life situation. One study, in the 1970's showed that a fatal heart attack often occurs in middle aged men about three years after a major disappointing life event. Examples included Nasser, leader of Egypt, after his failed attack upon Israel in 1967, and of Adlai Stevenson after he failed in his second attempt at the presidency against Dwight Eisenhower.

I have found that it is important to separate feelings of hopelessness from feelings of helplessness, which is far more common and can be treated differently. Hopelessness is most often a family trait, a prevailing feeling state carried over to young adulthood and that tends to become more pronounced with time. Many children and young adults try to defend against falling into feelings of hopelessness, which their parents may have created in the atmosphere of their childhood, by constantly acting upbeat, being busy, feigning enthusiasm, or trying to cheer others up. Hopelessness can predispose to suicide, especially if there is a family history of suicide. Feelings of hopelessness are not necessarily related to life events. It may be the presenting symptom of a genetic predisposition toward depression and an antidepressant medication should be prescribed on a trial basis. When the feelings of hopelessness, which are physiologically based, have somewhat abated, then the work of guidance can be more consistently and willingly practiced. That being said, there is no state that divine intervention of itself cannot improve.

Helplessness is a far more common feeling in this age of complexity and stress. It can follow a series of adverse events or a major loss. It is aggravated by fatigue and loss of sleep, and is often associated with self-blame and a lack of loving support. Here, surrendering to the feeling of helplessness and asking for higher help can lead to impressive results. I remember vividly the experience of a depressed woman who dreaded to face each day. She had to drag her children out of bed, get them dressed for school, prepare their breakfast and lunches, prepare her husband's lunch and record his list of chores that he wanted her to do that day. All the while she had to fight against passive-aggressive resistance, criticism, complaints, and a lack of appreciation. One day, after everyone had left the house, she fell down exhausted upon the living room couch exclaiming, "God help me." "I surrender." "I give up" She fell into a heavy sleep and awakened a few hours later much refreshed and with a different attitude. She continued to maintain this attitude of surrender and the atmosphere of her home soon changed dramatically thereafter.

Q. *God, what counsel do you have for those who have suicidal feelings?*

A.   All humans were created as free spirits and who have retained a natural urge to struggle against any form of limitation. The physical body can be very limiting and represents the cross you bear in completing your special mission on planet earth. None of you can comprehend the purpose and the value to the universe of even a seemingly insignificant life. You are a multidimensional being focused upon a miniscule body that has no sense of its own grandeur in the scheme of things, like the piece of a gigantic jigsaw puzzle that is incomplete without you, and that your thoughts create ripples that vibrate throughout the universe. No one is exempt from an occasional desire to give it all up. But, when you feel that your burdens are so heavy that you cannot possibly continue any further, take one more step as a special gift to Me.

Most people go to a psychiatrist to find a safe place to express their emotional pain. Usually they are seeking simple solutions for relief rather than answers that require them to radically change their behavior. But before behavioral change can occur, they need to recognize the link between their emotions and their thoughts. Most people have an undisciplined mind that has lost control of the thoughts that keep recycling judgments about themselves and everything else. Thus, we have become a drug-oriented society. Billions of dollars are spent each year by the Western world on medications, not including alcohol and street drugs, which are manufactured for the primary purpose of stopping the brain from thinking. However, the process of asking questions and asking for help is an essential step toward freeing you from becoming mechanically controlled by your environment.

Ask for the energy to overcome your feeling of tiredness. Ask for help in stopping the flow of depressive thoughts that keep you feeling a sense of lack and of helplessness. Remember that most emotions need specific statements to sustain them. Make new statements to yourself that will bring the emotions that you want. Also your own expectations have the power to make you feel excited and energized or else tired and discouraged. Remember that even unpleasant emotions can become an energy path to growth. Instead of finding ways to free yourself from unpleasant emotions, dare to experience them fully while offering them up to God for help, whether you understand their source or not.   You will be surprised how your patience and trust will be rewarded by a gradual and, permanent positive shift.

It is important for you to know the power of your thoughts. It is equally important for you to know that you need help in sorting your thoughts, to empower them with desire, and to extend them out with conscious will. Doubt, conflict, guilt, and unworthiness negate this process. Your family beliefs, the educational system, and the atmosphere and values of the society in which you were born can put you into a state of confusion out of which you spend the remainder of your lifetime redefining and declaring who you really are. You have to learn to listen inside for the answers instead of outside. As the good fairy said to Dorothy in the Wizard of Oz, "You always had the answer." "You haven't stopped to notice."

When to Ask for Help

You should, ideally, be asking for help all of the time, even when you think that things are going smoothly. However, there are obvious times when you feel absolutely miserable and don't know what to do about it. The place of comfort that your Intellect is constantly seeking has been shattered. There is no way to feel comfortable with food, drink, or television when you are feeling bad about yourself or angry over people saying or doing derogatory things behind your back. This feeling is not always brought on by just bad news, but by your agonizing over things that you have been criticized for doing wrong . Your "act" isn't working, and other people, or a special person you really care about isn't happy with you, and you don't know what to do about it.

Understand that all feelings go through change. Everything changes with time. Despair can be like a state of grace in which the ego has left the door wide open for the voice of the "Helper" to enter. It is time to consider the energy that you have been radiating and spreading around your environment for the past few days. Notice how things always tend to become more and more like you predicted they would. Be sure that you are not projecting energy out there that is going to come back to hurt you.

Ask God to ease the discomfort of those you may have hurt or offended, and an opportunity will come to make amends. The most common scenario is when you feel you have unnecessarily hurt someone's feelings or that someone is angry with you because of a misunderstanding. When you are lonely, confused, overwhelmed and under emotional stress your desire, sincerity and intent to make contact for help is greatly increased. In fact, God is not offended when your approach begins with anger. Bring your anger to God instead of unloading it upon a friend or family member. Write out your grievances, even if it takes a couple of pages. That will begin a flow of energy that is needed for change. Then listen!

Answers that come to you will be given in a way that you can understand and will accept. At first they may seem simple, almost "obvious", yet they will have a certain quality about them that is not your own ordinary way of thinking. Gradually, information may become more complex as you are gently lead to new levels of awareness. You may be surprised to find how relatively easy it is to reach God, because you are not separate from God's mind. No one can begin to solve the myriad of problems that the world appears to present. The youth of today are filled with questions begging for answers to their problems. No matter how many answers you may offer there are always more questions to follow. That is because the world has forgotten the only question that needs to be asked: "How do I make the connection to my Higher Self?"

The Role of God as "The Helper"[1]

There must have been many times when you wished that you had a "savior" who could lead your through the maze and confusion of your life. Trying to find this savior in another physical being never works for long. God serves as your personal Helper waiting for your call and your willingness to put aside your struggling Intellect and to listen. At first the voice is faint, but gradually grows stronger with use. It is not heard as a distinct voice but comes in the form of a new thought, an inspirational idea, or a revelation.

Your head is always filled with thoughts. Where do these thoughts come from? I have spent several years undergoing personal psychoanalysis only to discover that they are nothing more than meaningless voices from the past. They were useful for me to examine only for the purpose of understanding why my life kept going in repetitive circles. Since your thoughts determine your feelings and behavior, why not listen to the thoughts that come from a Source of knowing that gives a fresh meaning to every moment? It takes some practice to bypass the busy and argumentative thoughts that now run through your head and to listen to the thoughts of the Helper that come from a higher and intuitive level of knowing.

Gradually, trust will develop that someone or something is running your life from a higher level. The Helper or the "Holy Spirit" is the means by which God communicates with each of us from within our own heads. Once you begin the practice of examining your thoughts, you will begin to discern that they originate from many levels. You will gradually be able to dismiss the negative thoughts that arise from the past and that result in feelings of regret, depression, and guilt and, instead, consciously choose those thoughts that are uplifting and which serve you best. With help you will be able to choose only those thoughts that come from the highest Source, reminding you of your birthright to happiness and joy.

I have worked with many people from different religious backgrounds, including Muslim, Jewish, Hindu, and a variety of Christian denominations. None of them have ever objected to my referring to the functions of the Paraclete, Comforter, Good Shepherd, or Helper that Jesus promised He would send to us in the Holy Bible: John, verses 13-17. Following is an elaboration of those functions that I have accumulated over time from personal experience and from talking to others. It may require months or years to appreciate the full significance of all of them, but you can start with the ones that are most important to you today.

1. Ask God to monitor your thoughts and to detoxify the negative energies associated with your present personality such as anger, jealousy, blame, selfishness, and long held grievances.

2. Ask God to heal the grief, guilt, regrets, and wounds in your subconscious mind from the past. (Lie down and allow pictures to come to your mind that you would like to release by first forgiving yourself and then forgiving all of the other players on the stage of your life.)

3. Ask God to increase your patience, courage, and perseverance to undertake the challenges of life that are placed before you, and to be able to do it, not only with willingness, but even joyfully.

4. Ask God to guide your life into a meaningful direction filled with purpose, creativity, and satisfaction. (Use the following prayer: "God, open the doors that are meant to be opened and close the doors that are meant to be closed.")

5. Ask God to increase your sense of appreciation so that you can become a consistent energy vibration of inspiration in your communications with others.

6. Ask God to free you from all of the habits and addictions that do not serve your best interests.

7. Ask God to enhance your awareness so that you can see all of your problems from a new perspective that gives them special meaning as a crucial part of your life experience.

8. Ask God to help you to rise above your limited intellectual belief system and to offer positive alternatives to the fearful belief system of your parents that you have adopted.

9. Ask God to bring a positive transformation of memories, attitudes, and beliefs that begins to open your eyes to a new world, now thinly veiled, but far different from the world that you now see.

10. Ask God to release the pressure you put upon your Intellect to remember and to understand everything. Instead, adopt the wonderment of a child that will allow inner feelings to inspire a more sensitive awareness of life. You do not have to resolve all of your problems to move on.

11. Ask God to help make more active and real in your daily life, the image of the Ideal that you hold within yourself.

12. Ask God to release you from your guilt of the past and to shield you from the judgments and the opinions of others.

13. Ask God to open your heart, to improve your immune system, your emotional tranquility, and your physical and mental health.

14. Ask God to become a channel for the healing of others.

---

[1]the word, "Helper" , was inspired by the book of that title by Catherine Marshall, Avon Books, 1979

4

Patient Contributions

How do psychotherapists handle the many questions that are brought to them each day?

- •What is the meaning of my childhood suffering?
- •What purpose does pain play?
- •What can I do about the responsibilities and guilt that overwhelm me?
- •What more can I do for my children?
- •How do I get out of this horrible rut that I feel in my present life situation?
- •What do I do when I feel lonely, sad, depressed and everything is going wrong?
- •What purpose does my life have?
- •What do I have to look forward to?
- •Why am I chronically tired?
- •What is the cause of my anxiety attacks?
- •What do you do when giving turns into resentment?
- •How can I find time in my work to play?

The therapist must listen carefully in order to respond in a way that will be useful to the questioner. There is always some resistance to facing one's inner truth because every adult, as a child, has made silent contracts with their parents to be unaware of their parents' fears and limitations and to suppress thoughts and feelings that are different from those of their parents. The most effective therapist is one who has the most open view of the purpose and meaning of life. There is always the tendency to close the door on others that you have closed shut within yourself. That is what parents do to their children, and that is why people seek therapy. A therapist cannot normally guide another person any further along the road than he/she has traveled. However, through the practice of encouraging the handing over of all enquiries to God or the Indwelling Self, the inspired insights of the patient may lift the therapist, as well, to a new level of understanding.

Following are some shared examples of those who experienced dramatic changes in their life after following the practice of "Talking to God."

Mary Ann's Story

Mary Ann came to me as a tired looking, depressed and overwhelmed housewife, with a disabled husband that she felt obliged to support by working long hours in a high pressured job as a sales representative. She appeared older than her stated age. Her major problem appeared to be a lack of self-worth. When I asked her the primary reason why she had come to see me she exclaimed, "My life has to change."

After seeing her for a few sessions to help her to clarify specific details regarding the pattern of her life, it became clear that she was stuck in a feeling that dated back to early childhood of expecting and of receiving very little. Her father had left her mother during her pregnancy, and this contributed to a lifelong feeling of guilt for being born. Her mother had to work very hard and could not give her very much attention. When she did, it was always with a sense of impatience. She had never felt a sense of support or of peace. She had a religious background of weekly attending a church that preached about a judgmental God who saw everything as "good" or "bad." When I described my practice of teaching people to talk to God she stated that, "People tend to pray in a greedy way. I don't know what is appropriate to ask for." I suggested that she bring to God the same questions that she had brought to me. She obliged me, somewhat hesitantly, and was surprised that she actually received an answer that offered something more than just a repeat of what I had already discussed with her.

Q. God, why am I always so tired and depressed? Why do people take advantage of me at work?

A. You are trying too hard to conform to the world around you, which you have created. You have trained other people how to treat you. As you change, so will other people in your life.

I gave her the assignment of writing a sentence or two to God every morning upon awakening and to ask for energy to get through the day. Mary Ann happened to be a very self-disciplined person who went to the gym to work out early every morning. She also had a high motivation to please me, but she still had great difficulty in finding time in her busy schedule to carry out her assignment. I reassured her that I expected her to initially meet with some resistance and suggested that I would be satisfied with just an account of her general process of trying to write to God. Finally, she came to a session with a large smile on her face to turn in her "assignment":

> It was hard to put pen to paper the first time. I was taught to look at God as an aloof high being. I couldn't believe that He would actually relate to me in my every day problems. I was resistant for about three months. I bought a plain notebook to write in. I saw writing as a task. It was hard to just write and let it flow. I had to let my mind entertain the whole idea for several weeks to just accept the possibility. I didn't really understand it, but I developed a willingness to try, not as a "have to," but as a possibly enjoyable thing to do. At first it felt like it was my mother forcing me to play the piano when I didn't have the interest or talent. I had to believe it was something I actually could do.
>
> Then I decided to let go and see what would happen. I focused upon a bright six-pointed star above my head to

give me a source to communicate with. Now it flows so easily it's unbelievable. It began as a general journal to get the energy flowing, just talking to myself about my desire to grow and to know more about who I am and about God. I had to find quality time to do it. Just one more thing to do! I finally decided that I needed to take the time for me. After about two weeks, I made my first entry, "Dear God". I told Him all my problems, like He was someone I could give them all to. I complained about the stress in my life and the problems I was having with my job. For a week or two, I just wrote: " Good morning, God...." and did all the talking. I was surprised how my thoughts began to flow. It allowed me to get a fresh perspective and understanding of what I was going through. It's like a whole process of getting to know yourself and what you really think and feel. It did help to go through the list of affirmations you gave to me first, and then to become centered upon the heart. Somehow just talking to God about my problems seemed to resolve them. Solutions often occurred to me as I wrote about them. It feels much different from writing a report or even email. It just flows out.

Soon Mary Ann started talking to God while commuting to work and began to feel that Someone was listening. She slowly began to attract new things to herself. A wonderful new job opportunity opened up. She exclaimed, " I am feeling more like flowing in

the stream instead of constantly driving the water wheel to keep
the stream going. It's all about reclaiming myself. I was like a
peacock that was afraid to open my feathers." As her energy
level changed, she actually began to look much younger. She
was happy to offer some suggestions that might help others to
get started writing or talking to God:

Samples From Mary Ann's Journal Over The Past Year

I initially had no idea what I wanted when I walked into your
office. I thought life was too complicated to ever feel a sense
of peace. I always tried hard to make other people happy, trying
to create a moment that's not going to happen. Writing my
journal has been like an evolution of slowly waking up to who I
am. I had to take time to do things for myself and learn to say
"no" more often and in the right way. I was a performer without
an identity, filled with admonitions like:

> I'm not good enough.
> The world is against me.
> I have to please others.
> I can't really ever make it,
> Or be worthy of love.

Now I know that joy and happiness come from day in and day
out living. If you truly live your life the way you want to live
it, its not that difficult.

Q. Dear God, A new journey lies ahead for me. The door is open and I am seeing things clearly, and new options are opening up every day. I need to remember that You are with me always to check the turbulence in my own world. Tell me how I should face this day.

A. You should follow your heart for once. Your eyes are beginning to see more clearly; don't be afraid to keep them open. You must believe in yourself. Explore the world with the new eyes of Mary Ann that wants to shape her own destiny, the Mary Ann that sees clearly and makes choices of what she wants, the Mary Ann that can heal herself of all turbulence and live in a peaceful place within herself.

Q. Dear God, I have been in a state of not wanting to see. Sometimes, of course that is not true. It just eats away at me. Why do I do that?

A. It is a pattern of your past. If you don't feel, you won't have to find out the real truth. It is scary to look within, and it takes real work and persistence. It is like climbing a high mountain. It can be tiresome, but when you reach the peak, it gives you a sense of exhilaration. You just have to begin by putting one foot in front of the other, and trust that I will be there with you.

Q. God, You showed me another sign this morning. Why do I want to make myself suffer uselessly? What is in my make-up to do this?

A. It's an old tape, Mary Ann, a tape your mother played in her life, a tape you saw and called your own.

Q. Why do I push everyone away when I am in a crisis?

A. This is also another tape your mother gave to you. You noticed, when you were with her this weekend that she took out her anger against one of her friends on all of you. She doesn't know how to deal with her anger so she makes herself as miserable as possible. She makes herself suffer. She doesn't understand that her suffering doesn't solve her problems, but only intensifies them. Get out of your funk, Mary Ann. You don't have to wait until you're forty to be happy.

Q. God, I'm beginning to get back on track. I am trying to break out of my cocoon of self-pity. Why do I go there?

A. As I have said before, it is a habit that you are learning to break. It's something that protected you in the past, and now you use it as an avoidance technique. You have to become more aware of when you are in that cycle so you don't stay in the cesspool for so long.

Q. God, I have got myself depressed again. I feel like I'm not moving forward. The stress of my everyday tasks is consuming me. Help me to let go of the angst in my head. How do I do it?

A. You are using a lot of energy focusing upon the obstacles that you see in your life rather than just seeing them and taking them a little at a time. Your lesson is to learn to flow with the changing events in your life and to move through your fears. Just focus on one step at a time. You are learning to stand up for yourself, but remember that in doing so you are changing the way that people react to you. Don't be afraid, as you have in the past, to show your "peacock feathers." If your intention is good, you need not worry about the consequences of your actions. Energy changes always bring initial feelings of discomfort and resistance as you release the toxins that have resulted from hiding from yourself the thoughts and pain of the internal torture of your Iinner Core. Take a few minutes each day to center yourself. You are ready to emerge from the tunnel of your previous darkness, but you are afraid because you can't see the light and can't get rid of the excess baggage of others that you still carry around. Pause to bring My calmness into your body and Soul every day. Ask Me for help in relieving your feelings of discomfort.

Q. God, how am I doing? Could you review what You have been teaching me?

A. To work and be in the present moment. To let your life be easy and carefree. To feel the joy of life with Me. Let all the other things go! Don't get involved or say things that don't truly add to your life and the lives of others. Work on being your ideal women. Be sincere with your fellow human beings, be truthful and keep your promises to yourself. Understand that you create your day-to-day happiness. So be happy, stay in the present moment with Me. If you do that, life will easier.

Q. Dear God, we have made it through the week. I am still working on keeping focused, on keeping on track. How can I keep doing this?

A. As you know, it comes from a well deep within yourself, a place where your ego doesn't get involved, and a place of your true center of peace. Can you feel that place of peace inside where you can easily find Me? I am down there in that center. When you truly live with Me daily in and day out, your life becomes smooth. You are centered in Me, therefore centered in life. You become one with Me and at peace with yourself. You have no fears because I am with you. You have no malice because thats not you or Me. You understand the source of the light within you and can clearly see your evolution in you. Once you find Me in you, everything else falls into place.

Mary Ann would like to offer others the following suggestion :

"You have to take all the fear away first. No one is going to grade you on this. You have to see it as a joyful activity. In fact, I sometimes felt that my inner child began asking some of the questions. There's a flow of energy associated with it. The availability of it is very exciting. It helps you to realize that your patterns create the patterns around you. Give yourself a chance. It's something like finding a truest friend. It's always there for you, and helps you to stop listening to the internal tapes. This opens you up to the beautiful things in the world. I no longer awaken stressed at night. It helps you to discover you. You're always left with you."

Lynette's Story

Writing has always been something I knew I had a desire to do, and I felt good when I wrote. But I've always been waiting for the right time to feel the right way, and of course it needed to be perfect, without errors in grammar, spelling or anything else. It had to be just right. Well, waiting around for that to happen will take forever.

Writing the questions and answers and other things these past few weeks has been freeing in that I just did it without caring if it was right or not. It felt great and it also felt like a waste of time, but I did it because I told myself it was an assignment that had to be done, good or not. I just defied the voices and wrote without a lot of thought. As a result I've felt empowered and felt that I have something to say. There's been a fight inside me, wanting to feel good on my own, or waiting to get praise or approval from the outside world. I realize the habit of waiting for everything to be just right will never happen, and that I need to just start even if it's for no other reason than because I want to and it feels good.

Q. What should I write about and from what angle should I write?

A. You should write about what you know. You know about feelings, you know how to convey them, and you should write from a perspective of sharing them with someone who really wants to know about it and is interested in your questions.

Q. What events in my life should I write about first?

A. You should speak about the life events that bring up the most emotions for you at this time. Your emotions will carry your ideas and creativity.

Q. What part of my life brings up the greatest emotion in me at this time, and would be good for me to write about?

A. What was it like to be an invisible child with two parents who weren't there?

Q. Okay, I felt tired, bored, unmotivated, disappointed and lonely. The loneliness reminds me of all the Sundays I've spent feeling lonely and sad. But it's not Sunday, and yet the feelings are the same. Why do I feel so alone and isolated sometimes?

A. You have the energy of many belief patterns that were put into you at a cellular level and will take a lifetime to completely overcome. The fears you have are not yours. They come from other sources. Loneliness comes from a lack of communication, both inner and outer. Communication is the theme and forefront of everything else. You have come to believe that there is no one who wants to listen to you, and so you have not drawn these people into your life. Communication is one of the gifts I offer to you.

Q. How will I ever have and feel meaning in my life? Will I ever be happy and fulfilled?

A. In life there are many ups and downs and you certainly have had your share. But you are constantly changing, constantly growing, and are beginning to have a more even keel to your life. You are meant to be where you are at this time.

Q. Why do I feel down lately, so melancholy? Sometimes, I feel like crying, but I'm not sure if it's because I'm so happy or because I'm so sad.

A. There are many changes you are going through at this time. You are so happy to finally be finding yourself again, someone whom you have missed dearly, and yet the sadness is because you're seeing more and more clearly how your family has never been a real family to you. It is the sadness of knowing the reality of the lack of love in your life, and the family you never had, but tried so hard to pretend as if you did. Your life had been a struggle trying to find love and struggling with picking all the wrong partners. Reflect upon the miracles in your life that sustained you through the rough and painful times. The miracles have not been the life-saving kind, and yet nevertheless were lifesaving. Without one of these miracles you may very well have fallen into despair so great that recovery would be impossible.

Q. The talents I have, I have always just assumed everyone has and that they just had more control over using them.

A. The purpose of this assignment is for you to experience the nature of the healing which you have to give to other humans by looking to God for answers. You are a storyteller who can entertain and make people laugh. But you must be able to discern those whom you can benefit. A person asks a question. You answer briefly. They may want no further information. If they ask another question, then they want to know. So, it's for you to be more aware of how little information the average person really wants.

Q. Why do I feel so fearful and nervous inside, even though there is nothing particular to fear right now?

A. You are upon a new leap in growth, and all change brings fear. You must not resist the fear. Say "hello" to it. Face it and it will lighten. Find the source and tell it you have no use for it. Sometimes you just need to acknowledge the way you feel and embrace it.

Q. Why is it when I feel wonderful about myself that I also feel so afraid that I'm going to get into trouble?

A. Your parents could not tolerate the higher level of vibration that the happiness of a child radiates, and they tended to compulsively pull you back to their lower energy level of worry and fear. That is why you and so many people have never been allowed to discover their true selves that is a gift from God who has given each a uniqueness that is needed in the world.

Q. Why is it so hard to get beyond this?

A. The world that you see seems to have more power than you. And the emotions that come up become stronger as you try to resist them. You need to work with them instead of against them. When you find yourself in an uncomfortable state of mind, try to do something else you're good at. Don't try to see yourself as great, but just do something simple that you enjoy. It's like riding over uncomfortable emotions. Do not try so hard to do something that makes you feel good about yourself, or having something special happen that makes you feel good about yourself, which is a way of convincing yourself that you are special and deserving. Trying to convince yourself, and the world that says otherwise, won't work. You must just keep doing what feels good. Just keep doing what you do best no matter what, like giving to your children and knowing you're a good mom. Instead of lying down with a headache and giving in to the old voices, just let them talk while you're doing what you know will be good for you to do. Even if you're a bad tennis player doesn't mean you should give up tennis if you like to play the game.

Q. The answers I get are only satisfying for a short time. It is not like I get an answer and say – "Oh, yes, that's true. I believe it." – and then go on with a radical change in my beliefs and feelings. I think that was what I expected to happen, and why it's so hard to continue.

A. The answers may not be a cure in the short term. But if you keep asking the same questions and even if you keep getting the same positive answers, eventually they will override the old repetitive negative answers.

Jessica's Writings

I am feeling sad and hurt by all the male members of the law firm who don't like me or tolerate me because I'm a woman. Is it an ego thing? I feel like a misfit, impatient for a better life and environment, tired of all the hard work of the past. I want to have more time for travel, art, music, leisure time, gardening, working with children, and experience love. I want to resonate with the best part of each person, even though they are ugly. The hardest is even when they do not like me. I don't understand why I am in this situation.

> Q. Is this the lesson—that before I get to a higher plane of bliss and love, I need to learn that I have to be an instrument of love to even hateful people?

A. Yes, My dear one, you are beginning to see it. You do learn fast. All these lessons and events may feel overwhelming, but you have asked for and are ready for these lessons to come quickly and you are assimilating them quickly.

Q. Well, actually, that is something I am worried about. Am I really assimilating them so quickly? I mean, they go by so fast, I am afraid that I am not . . .

A. What, you want to suffer more!

Q. No! Not at all, but I guess I doubt my ability to have these lessons sink down to the Soul level.

A. All lessons are not learnt until they are at the Soul level and once they are, they become cognitively recognized. So, once it is at the point where you can cognitively say, "Aha," you know it at your Soul level. Is there any thing else that causes you concern?

Q. You make it seem so very easy.

A. It is. It is only that humans have this idea that they must suffer to achieve rewards and to bask in the joy of accomplishments. It was never meant to be so hard and it is NOT so hard!! You know this at a level that is coming closer to your cognition – see? All things are first known at the Soul level. Once they are recognized cognitively, you have got it!

Q. Aha!

A. Yes, you have got it, dear one.

Q. Should I change my job and go to another firm?

A. First, nothing really matters with respect to this inquiry about your job. In the long run, both are simply vehicles. Neither job, nor filling these jobs, will change the course of the events that you are to experience in coming years. You will gather the same experiences and data from whatever job you choose.

Q. So would it not be too presumptuous to ask how much longer I have to wait to arrive at the existence on this earth that I so very much desire – that is my heart's desire?

A. It is in the cards if you want it to be in the cards and it will not be if you don't. You may choose that point of view if you wish; you can have anything that you choose. It is really up to you and what you THINK! Those thoughts are most powerful as well that are coming from deep inside – the place that feels fear and anxiety and doubt. It is at a very deep level that you feel these things and may not consciously even think them.

Q. I want to purge myself of those thoughts if I can.

A. Are you certain?

Q. I think part of what is holding me back as well is mom and her negativity, her fear. I need to change that; I need to find a way to keep her influences away from me, not entering me.

A. Remember, do not judge. Think about how you would not have known the power of such influences had she not been your mother. How could you overcome them had you not been programmed by one whose inputs would be so powerful? How could you know your strength and faith in overcoming those fears had they not been present from the beginning, and at such a very basic level?

Q. I know, all she has is fear, concern regarding money, not having enough. Plus she is always telling me what to do.

A. Let it go, let it go and know that she does not influence you anymore in the least with respect to her fears.

Q. So what about me? How do I have time, abundance, expansiveness, space, freedom, and unfetteredness?

A. Do you really want this? When you are ready, it will simply be the result. It is as easy as that, as simple as that. Just as a hamster deciding to step off the wheel, you need to trust—you do not yet believe one hundred percent that all bills, the mortgage, etc. will be non-issues once you make the choice. This is very hard for you to let go of—like thinking you've been hanging from a rope over a bottomless cavern. And I am telling you that there is no cavern. It is an illusion. Let go of the rope. You are trusting your eyes and not your other senses. You will not let go. When you do, you will be surprised and delighted.

Q. But what about my responsibilities, like supporting my mother? There will be repercussions.

A. Once you let go, get off the wheel, others will see and believe more easily. You feel that you are the only resource to make others feel okay. They will be okay. If they will not be okay, you cannot—even with your desperate caring and love, will it to be so. They have their own ropes and caverns to which they are connected, but separate from you and your choices. So you must let it go—the concern for others, and the concerns about money, mortgages, whatever. Once you do, there is so much more to see and to be. Fear is your main problem. The only way to overcome fear is to make the connection to the Source of all power and all love. Your questions open up a relationship. Your questioning opens you up to receptivity. Your questions will lead to more questions and more questions because there is no final answer to your illusion of limitation and lack, and the experience that comes with trust and receptivity will open you up more fully to the Truth.

Q. OK. It is still a challenge. Can I write down a quote I want to remember?

A. You can write whatever you want; this is your dialogue.

Q. Okay, friends that mind don't matter and those that matter don't mind. So, thank You again. I can't wait! Thank You.

A. Go in blissful peace, Little One. You are right to appreciate yourself and to be pleased. It is the right feeling and We are also pleased. The situation is good and you are deserving of pleasure and of feeling pleased. Don't wait so long in between our talks.

Q. Okay!

Within one year a special opportunity opened up for Jessica. For the first time, she was able to say each day upon awakening each morning, "I love my job."

Laura's Contribution

Laura provides a good example for those who think that they have to receive long and detailed answers to their questions, such as some of the samples offered here. It is not so much the verbal content but the feeling that accompanies a response that we are seeking.

Laura is an attractive, youthful-appearing forty year old flight attendant who had never had a significant romantic relationship. She kept moving from one city to another because she never felt either comfortable or at home anywhere. The atmosphere of her childhood home was heavy with the depression of two chronically ill parents. Her brother committed suicide while in his teens. She didn't know what it was like to be happy. She tended to befriend depressed people and attempt to cheer them up. Although she did try to socialize, and occasionally went on group activities such as skiing trips, she wondered whether something was wrong with her because no eligible man had invited her out on a date for the past ten years. She did not appear outwardly depressed, but definitely lacked enthusiasm regarding her future. She had difficulty knowing what questions to ask, and it was equally difficult for me to know what answers she would accept.

During the course of therapy, I suggested that Laura try to write to God for some answers. She obliged, somewhat skeptically, and came to me the next session with a number of questions that she had written in a notebook. It was clear that she had accepted her family script of depression, and did not want either me or God to superficially cheer her up in the way that she was accustomed to do for others.   Every one of her half-dozen questions received a simple one-word answer of either, "Yes" or "No". Finally, she asked, "Can you answer me in longer sentences than just 'Yes' or 'No'?" She received the reply, "Yes, I can." I suggested that she ask, "What is the most important thing that I should focus upon now?" She did so, and received, "The color yellow." She did not understand the significance of this until I explained that yellow was the color of her emotional center in the solar plexus. Essentially, it is the realm of the inner child. She needed to release her playful inner child and learn to enjoy the beauty of nature. The inner child, when unencumbered by a weighty Intellect, expresses an effervescent energy like that of a child splashing and shouting while at play in a wading pool. The life force flows through the inner child when not held down by depressive thoughts.

I taught Laura how to put her hands on her belly and to speak to her inner child and to assume a more playful attitude toward life. The next session she brought in a dream of her being a dolphin in a small swimming pool. I helped her to see that she was being shown the nature of her dilemma. I had her go back into the dream, and we worked upon digging a tunnel from the bottom of the pool out to the open sea. The subconscious mind responds to this type of symbolism even more than to words.

Her life has since begun to change as she is becoming more vibrant from the feeling of a new sense of freedom from her past.

Lynne's Questions

Lynne was the only child of a very brittle and immature mother who had been raised in an orphanage. She had to be the perfect little girl, very much like a cute and sweet little doll that could not express feelings. She had to restrict all of her physical and emotional energies, be totally available and predictable, and have no complaints or needs of her own. She would never dare to question or to threaten her insecure mother in any way. Her father loved her but was afraid to show it. She had to constantly placate her mother's abandonment fears and never allowed herself to be aware of her true feeling when she disliked her mother for fear that she would end up being abandoned by her. She went through life trying to make everyone around her feel comfortable by being sweet and helpful. This did not gain her the respect she wanted, and she came to me depressed because her life was not working. She had a boyfriend that she was in danger of losing because she clung so tightly to him due to her jealousy and her fear of abandonment when he was not constantly by her side.

We had many sessions before I suggested that Lynne ask God to answer some of the issues that she had raised. Although her problem appeared clear to me, I had difficulty breaking through the "firewall" of her ego defenses in order to bring about a real change in her life. She had also taken numerous growth workshops over the years but she had never allowed any of them to sink below the level of her surface Intellect in order to permit herself to expand her self-concept to that of a mature woman. However, her ability to make communication with her inner Self was impressive, and this marked the beginning of a dramatic shift in her self-concept and, eventually, her outer behavior.

Q. God, I still have issues around my trust and relationship to men. How can I change this?

A. Men also have basic needs and desires that are common to women, although there may be different ways of expressing these needs, and through the ages the roles of men and women have been very different. In your childhood dream your daddy was a fallen hero. He is very sad about that. If you could now tell him that you understand and forgive him, he will hear and you will be released. A point of maturity and empowerment comes when you can forgive your parents for being human. By forgiving your father you release your anger at men in general. They are all guilty by association in your mind at some level.

Q. God, I want my voice, my body, my sensuality felt in dancing and movement. Now that I know that you are in every cell of my body it gives me permission to integrate my spiritual self with my physical self. This is a big deal for me. Any comment on how to keep this moving?

A. One step at a time. Remember it is about Being, not doing. There is nothing to do. When you start doing your intuition shuts down. That part gets overwhelmed. Eventually as your intuition is given more space to be, you will be able to make faster shifts from doing to being. You have prayed to feel Me in every cell of your body. I am there so touch Me and feel Me everywhere. There is not a bodily function that I am not in. Touching yourself and feeling Me will heal the shame you learned of touching your body as a child.

Q. I was very upset by Margie's attention to my boyfriend this weekend. What can I learn from this?

A. You are reacting with fear. Your fear is that someone will try to take your boyfriend away from you and you will be helpless like you were with mommy. You felt helpless when she wanted daddy's attention, and she just took it. You are not so helpless now. You have had affairs with several different men. You were acting out of that same space of proving that you finally had power.

It is not to say that there was not some love there, but you were driven by the impulse to "win the man."

Q. How can I keep You alive in me today? I am afraid I will forget the experience of my session this week.

A. It is about slowing down, quieting down, something like a metronome that moves more slowly. It's not that either fast or slow is better. It is appropriate to move fast at times. It is just that to find Me and connect with Me—like a friend—you can't be rushing in and out of your body. I am in your body, in your heart and Soul and every cell in the breath. I am out there too but you first must connect inside. Stop for even a short moment to notice Me. Look for me everywhere - in a flower - in a tree - in people. Look for me with the intention of connecting with a friend. Look at everything with the intention of finding Me. Make it like a game. I am everywhere so it's a game you can't lose.

Q. What do I need to know to feel my connection to You?

A. Know that I am you and you are Me. Feel Me in your heart through the breath. When you breathe it is a reminder that I am there. Enjoy. Be the joy of life.

Q. I need to have some words to make me feel closure and reassurance. What should I have learned from this recent crisis at work in which I felt helpless and frustrated? What was the lesson in it for me?

A. This lesson was for you to really experience the angry undeveloped emotions that are rampant in the world. If you are going to be a teacher, you have to know fully what you are dealing with. You have to learn to deal with these emotions in yourself in order to deal with them out there.

Q. How do I become less reactive to people like this? I am usually put into a position of being disrespected or powerless no matter how hard I try.

A. You thought that just being sweet and having good intentions would be enough. In the world this is looked upon as weakness. Showing sweetness and good intentions were very important tools to you as a child, but to do battle in the world you have to learn the skills to deal with that which is not what you wish it to be.

Q. I still don't understand what I have been doing wrong.

A. You need the tools to go along with your heart and your intentions to be fully powerful in the world. Your feelings of powerlessness have to do partly with your lack of skills and understanding. You need both. A more mature perspective is important: 1.) Be more aware of whatever you do, think, and feel, 2.) Tell the truth to yourself, and 3.) Take responsibility for your thoughts as well as your actions. You have My support.

Martha's Experience

Martha isa middle-aged, married Jewish woman who was suddenly faced with a number of seemingly unrelated negative events in a relatively short period of time. This had the effect of forcing her to question the direction and purpose of her life. She was a very serious and conscientious person and, yet, through no obvious fault of her own, she found herself the subject of discrimination and attack at the school where she taught, by neighbors that had recently moved in next door, and by members of her own family for some seemingly harmless remarks that she had made. She also had not been feeling physically well for some time. She was beginning to believe that God was against her, so I persuaded her to confront Him directly. I am summarizing her several weeks of questioning here:

Q. I have had so many negative things happen to me this past year that I feel that the universe is trying to punish me for something.

A. The fact that you have had a lot of negative experiences or have expressed considerable negative thoughts in the past does not mean that you cannot turn everything around at any age. Examine the negative imprints about other people that you put into your mind in the past and which you are now reexperiencing.

The past is not the future. You are not bad. You may have needed these experiences to know what it is you really want. There is no judgment, only learning. It is like a sign seen on the U.C. Berkeley Campus: "Been there, done that!" There is less danger now of repeating past mistakes. Let go of guilt, blame, or judgment. You are not here to pay back anything done badly. One thing that could be of value is a strengthening of self-validation regardless of how you are judged by any external source. It is an opportunity to look deep within and say, "Suppose I were a magnet or a boomerang sending out energy with every thought or pulse beat of my heart, what would be the nature of that? Is it every moment caring, loving and healing? What stream is coming from my belly area?" Those who see beyond the earth see energies going out in a looped fashion. Someone says, "You are a selfish being." You must retort, "I am really a loving being." Then what is sent out will eventually return.

Q. How do I let go of deep resentments from what is imposed upon me by others, including family members?

A. Don't obsess over whether others suffer from their offenses against you. The amount of pain and the mindset of injustice are difficult to break. If you could immediately make every person who offended you suffer, you would still move with a sense of emptiness and lack of direction. This would not awaken the feeling of joy. The healing can only come from within.

Q. How to do that in a practical sense?

A. Where circumstances have given you every reason to be bitter, the ultimate revenge is being happy and truly at peace so that abundance may return to you. You cannot impose a system of thinking upon other people. Release others to think, as they will. You are not responsible for their incorrect invalidation. What you need to focus on is what you need to send out. Your inner joy is unassailable by outer circumstances.

Q. What is my purpose?

A. The purpose of every Soul upon the planet is to make joy the dominant experience of life. Every bit of laughter or gratefulness ripples out to the multidimensional universe and never stops. Any consciousness wanting to participate can be drawn into this energy on other dimensions. In the process of growth there is the necessity of each consciousness in the universe to understand that which <u>is</u> by experiencing that which <u>is</u> <u>not</u>. Darkness is not something tangible. No one walks into a room to turn on the <u>dark </u>switch. You experienced this life because of the gain that will far outshadow the misery suffered. It is something like boot camp or a strenuous training to reach an athletic prime. There are moments that are hated, even times when you may wonder why you ever agreed to undertake it. But the moment of graduation has a sweetness that makes it all worthwhile. Another example is ice skaters going through a grinding training. If interviewed moments before participating in a major world competition, they might express primarily feelings of stress or, perhaps, nervous impatience until after they have tasted the joy of performing with coordination and applauded grace. The joy after the moment of a special achievement brings a shift from the feelings of the moments preceding it.

Q. But how do I begin to make this change?

A. By being happy, appreciative, and receptive.
   By releasing all old resentments.
   By anticipating benefits, for even those things that
      seem at the time as failures
   By expecting good things to happen.
   By finding something deliberately every day to give
      you pleasure.

Anything that focuses your energy into a positive aspect, no matter how small or seemingly insignificant it is, the intention, the willingness to smile, accept, and forgive is what matters. If you would participate in God's joy of creation, then learn to extend yourself. Know the difference between extension and projection. Let your giving be a joy to others and not a debt they owe you. Begin asking, "Who am I?"

Martha was a mature Soul who was able to see that she was being forced by her own higher Self to move out of a period of relative isolation and stagnation in her life by shifting her energies to a new level and then to extend them more effectively into her environment.

Steve's Experience

Steve had the problem of frequently waking up in the middle of the night replaying the previous day and wondering whether he was doing everything right. "Life is not fun!" He made a good salary but he gave himself away to get respect and money. He began to feel a heavy shield over his body. "It feels like me trying to come out." He felt anger like a tight knot in his head and at the root of his nose. Fear cast a dark shadow on the left side of his head. There was constant effort and intensity with no sense of naturally flowing. He was amazed that the answers came when he began to ask. He had to acknowledge first that he didn't know what to do. He had to reprogram the conflict around making money. He complained of burning in his stomach from the fear of being wrong. He began writing on a daily basis.

Q. *What is my resistance to knowing what to do and feeling unable to reconnect?*

A. Fear keeps you from letting go of learned preconceived notions about people and about what matters. Your identity is tied into the negativity of the past. Your father suddenly abandoned the family and your mother never permitted you to question what she was thinking or feeling. You were never allowed a role in any type of decision-making and had to be a "good boy" who never questioned what you were told. Can you understand how this now cripples your ability to make decisions or to even gather the necessary information that you need?

Q. *How do I control my fear and stop listening to the tapes in my head?*

A. Your Intellect is too cluttered. Feeling that you have Higher support is the key to moving on. Open up to receive Me and you will be free. It is like non-verbal healing. Your connection will show you the way if you remain simple and open. You must attempt to establish a rhythm every day. There's no need to worry. Always be open to knowing. Be open to all things and you will be able to control all things. It's okay to take everything in. You can't feel compassion until you stop beating yourself up. Don't be afraid to move out of the comfort zone.

Q. I always feel alone. I am afraid of being rejected or abandoned.

A. You are not lonely when you are engaged in doing something you like and enjoy doing. Omit activities that keep you from your goal of being happy. Express the openness of being alive, being there, the continuity of being in that time and space where you can enjoy being there. Once you start, you've taken your biggest step. Then let it flow. Be a part of what you want. Doing what you know in your heart is the secret to becoming connected. You must do this every day.

Q. I never felt totally understood or totally loved. When the tape is playing, I can't be in that place.

A. Open the heart and mind and allow the light in. The understanding is there. The joy comes from letting the power you have within come out. The Father enjoys your allowing yourself to do this. There is the fear that it won't work. It works by doing it! The Intellect interferes. Opening to other Intellects will close down and suppress the energy. Your feelings of sorrow come from the overshadowing of your creative energy by the Intellect. It keeps you from feeling complete.

Q. What can I do about my doubt and fear of making decisions and talking to strangers?

A. Decide what it is you would like to be able to do without fear, and then demonstrate courage and will to override your fear. Expect success, visualize success, and develop the ability to overcome subconscious programming of doubt and limitation. List purposely the things that you have some discomfort doing, and then set aside a definite time for doing each in a way in which you would want someone that you had hired to do it. Your personality evolves out of your present actions and intentions and motives. Your identification with the past keeps you chained there. Practice saying to yourself: "I am a different person today than I was yesterday." Your task is not to seek for love, but to seek and find all of the barriers within yourself that you have built up against it.

Q. I can feel the resistances. What I want is wrong somehow. I can't be myself. They won't like me. I gave value to the voices inside my head. I'm afraid to be a dreamer. It is like standing on the edge of a high diving board. How do I make the jump from them to me? I must leap from the diving board into my core Self. I need a push. I won't allow myself because I don't own myself.

A. Begin to feel a place within where conflict does not exist. Feel more anchored. It's time to cut the shit! It's time to learn who the real Steve is. Every morning think about the day you want. Learn to embrace controversy by doing a heart check: "Is this what I really want?"

Q. What activity should I move toward to find more satisfying work?

A. Try just about anything that attracts you. JUST DO SOMETHING SOON!

Just before this book went to print, Steve began to feel a shift in his energy and began to notice that people at work began to honor him more. He wanted to share what he finally learned at a deeper level: "You have to allow yourself to be who you are. You have to dare to know that you want something different and you have to be willing to live in the pain until the change occurs."

Sarah's Story

One young, attractive unmarried Moraccan woman who was working on a technical research project in a highly pressured setting came to me complaining that her life was emotionally sterile. She had attained a Ph.D. through her studies in prestigious institutions of learning in several different countries. She spoke at least five languages fluently, and still felt that she had no real roots. Her main complaint was loneliness and disenchantment with life. Her mother was a very unhappy woman who prayed religiously every day without any discernable change in her circumstances. Thus, Sarah was skeptical about praying and remained wholly unaware of her spiritual resources. I explained that writing to God was somewhat different than what her mother had done mechanically each day and that it was more like talking to a caring mentor from whom she could expect answers. She remained skeptical, but was willing to oblige me.   Because she was a Muslim, I encouraged her to address Allah for answers to her questions. She resisted this because her personal feeling about Allah was that He was a "macho God" and that she preferred to address her Higher Self.

> *Q. Higher Self, Why am I here? What's my purpose? Why all the struggle? Where's the light? Are you there? Why do you put me through this?*

A. Sarah, I want you to know that life is worth living. Be patient and you will see the end of the tunnel. You will be helped so you can help others later.

Q. *What's the next step? Where do I go from here?*

A. Doors will open.

Sarah felt discouraged by these simple answers, but I knew that there was really nothing else she needed to know at this time. She needed encouragement to persevere along the path she was going. She was not yet ready for a greater understanding that would help her to see the purpose of her life from a higher level. As we continued to work together, her awareness significantly increased. During the following weeks she reported that she had begun watching her thought patterns and that she had begun seeing her situation through new eyes. She had less need for constant approval and less fear of her supervisor. She remarked, "Seeing that others are not malicious, but just as insecure as I am, makes working with them more tolerable."

Then, Sarah's learning was accelerated, as is often the case, by her need to offer counseling to a young niece who called from Morocco and mentioned that she was having nightmares and depression. Sarah did a magnificent job in offering to her the understanding and reassurance that her niece needed, according to her recounting of their conversation to me.

Sarah's greatest fear was that she would lose her job at the research lab because of recent downsizing and that this would put her green card for temporary citizenship in jeopardy. Her Intellect was tired from seeking diplomas as a way of survival in a man's world. She had spent the holidays with an older sister and could see clearly how her sister was coping with a bad marriage and the feelings of being powerless as a woman by becoming unconscious to her feelings and focusing upon trite immediate goals such as finding a new hair stylist and buying some new items for her wardrobe.

I had Sarah lie down upon the couch to complain about her feelings of being a woman in the world to her Higher Self. I added that this required enough emotion to make ripples that would reverberate through the universe. She suddenly felt that everything that had been held inside since birth wanted to come out as a loud scream: "I don't want to be here." She needed to have that scream acknowledged. I encouraged her to allow the unexpressed parts of her body to speak out. With this came a release in the form of gurgling sounds within her belly that could be felt with my palm. I gave her the assignment of every day asking her Higher Self what she wanted in place of what she had.

Imagine my surprise when Sarah came to see me two weeks later with a smile on her face as she reported that she had just lost her job. Instead of fear, there was a sense of relief. She explained that she hated her job but didn't know what options she had. She now had a new feeling: that she had to go through this experience - to experience her greatest fear - and still feel comfortable. She had a sense of optimism about going through this "transition phase." Sarah had suddenly acquired a sense of trust in the universe and, with this, dared to go through the exercise every night of telling the universe what she wanted: "I want to detach from the past." "I want a change for the better." "I want to graduate from my internship of experiencing my old construct (personality pattern) and to be receptive to higher help." "I'm tired of using my left brain to try to cope, and want to use my intuitive right brain instead." One night, she had a dream of her mother dying and falling into a deep well. With this came a sense of relief as she realized that this meant that she was being freed from a large part of her mother's belief system about the world.

Sarah had "coincidentally" come across a catalogue from an accredited school of massage and felt an urge to take a beginning class there to use her right brain in order to experience her intuitive, feeling self. She had also found a support group in the other forty employees who were suddenly laid off from work like herself and who had agreed to meet regularly to discuss their options. Most important, Sarah was able to state with some conviction, that it really didn't matter what temporary job she found since she now sees that any job is just a vehicle toward her larger goal of expanding her consciousness and of feeling a connection to her Higher Self.

PART II

Gaining Mastery Over
Situations, Problems, and Crises

The Nature of Crises

5

Mastery Over Situations, Problems, and Crises

We can begin to learn how to eliminate problems, which seem to be such an integral part of our lives, when we understand the difference between 1.) Situations, 2.) Problems, and 3.) Crises.

1. Situations, as defined here, include the events, circumstances and changing conditions that are an ongoing part of everyone's everyday life experience. Life consists of a series of situations that require decisions as to how to best use one's time, material resources, and energy. New situations might be challenging and may require training and experience to resolve, but they always have a reasonable solution. An airplane pilot, for example, may encounter stormy weather, or an automobile driver may come upon heavy traffic on the way to work, but if the airplane pilot had proper training and the automobile driver had anticipated the traffic delay, neither would consider their particular situation to be a problem. Routine hassles, delays, and temporary frustrations usually fit into the category of "situations" because they are not associated with personal failings.

2. Problems, on the other hand, are a function of perception and are always linked to a distressing emotion. Problems may be related to health, money, work, relationships and a number of conditions that we tend to see as occurring outside of

ourselves. However, there is always a sense of personal attack or judgement associated with them. It is important to make a distinction between a normal or neutral situation and what we perceive to be a problem because situations can be settled while problems seem to recur despite our attempts to avoid them.

Problems are created by the mind, and *the mind that creates problems does not have the perspective to find permanent solutions to the problems it creates.* Situations can be resolved by appropriate education, training, or good advice; whereas problems are rarely amenable to advice because they are an inherent part of each person's personality make-up and thus must be taken to a Higher Source for a resolution.

3. Crises go beyond problems. They are experienced as unexpected catastrophic events that are totally out of our control and that can have a significant influence upon the direction of our life thereafter. We now know that many people who experience even one major crisis may subsequently suffer from the clinical diagnosis of "Post-Traumatic Stress Disorder." The special issues associated with crises are discussed in Chapter Six.

Why Problems Seem Inseparable From Life.

Problems begin from an early age when we are taught to judge and to label the changes occurring in our environment as either "good" or "bad," depending upon our attachment to them. From the moment we become self-conscious as an infant we become concerned about what others think about us and become dissatisfied with ourselves when we begin to compare ourselves with other seemingly more favored or successful people or siblings.

Almost without exception, every child, in every society, has been exposed to some type of limitation, lack, or abuse. The abuse does not need to be overtly physical or emotional. Just as hurtful to a child's self-image is the invalidation of his feelings. This is where our "problems" originate. We spend our lifetime trying to avoid feelings of lack, rejection, and abuse by trying to change the outer world to make us feel more secure, loved, and comfortable. Believing that we have to work hard to accomplish something important in order to be accepted, praised, and loved creates stress and can generate, in our mind, problems that have no end.

Problems are very personal experiences due to individual perceptions that differ only slightly with age. Most television sitcoms such as "Steinfeld," "Frasier," "Cheers," "I Love Lucy," and "Friends" consist primarily of people in different settings going through a series of repetitive problems that appear humorous to the viewer. The characterization of each actor or actress is defined by the unique types of problems that each creates and the inept ways in which they routinely attempt to solve those problems. Their efforts to find solutions either tend to create more problems or else set up the same "problem board" again and again. The audience predictably consists of individuals who experience similar problems and enjoy seeing others in the same dilemma.

Granted, there are serious circumstances facing many people in the world today that are related to war, prejudice, and man's inhumanity to man. These are created by the group mind, which Karl Jung labeled as archetypes. The reasons that we may be drawn into them and the part that we play on either side of the drama and why, is beyond the scope of this book.

That being said, we must not look entirely to outer circumstances as the main cause for our unhappiness. I interviewed several adults who were young children in England during WWII. Their activities were constantly interrupted by air-raid sirens that forced them to run to shelters because of the German V2 missile attacks upon their cities. I expected them to tell me that this was the most unhappy and frightening time in their lives. Instead, some exclaimed that these were actually memories that they cherished. They remember being held and comforted by their mother and family in the midst of a united group energy. To a child, love and caring matter more than anything else. It is not the external circumstances themselves that create problems, but the feelings we have about the circumstances.

There is one problem that all humans have in common, and that is their loneliness. We try to cover it up through busyness, "partying," and getting involved in "noble causes." But, eventually, it catches up with us. We are somewhat surprised when we read that even some of our favorite movie stars suffer from loneliness when off the stage.

To children, attention is equated with love, and being seen is the only way that they can feel "real". A young child can become preoccupied with curiosity and playing with crayons and toys in their playpen for only so long before they begin to experience a sense of loneliness. Nothing can substitute for a loving adult watching them at play and sharing their enjoyment. The adult doesn't necessarily have to do anything or teach the child how to play. Just active interest is enough. Without this there is a sense of a loss of connection to someone or to something that would make them feel whole. Children who do not have an appropriate amount of focused parental attention feel a sense of isolation. Many adults, as well, have told me of a recurrent dream of being "lost in a void" that can be traced to being invalidated or ignored as a child even when they were flooded with new toys to play with.

Young adults are constantly seeking the ideal relationship that will make them feel complete. But even when they believe that they have found this in another person (and the experience may, indeed, be a very important touchstone for them to cherish and to remember), the incompleteness of any relationship with another physical being makes it virtually impossible to indefinitely fill their need for a constant sense of importance and security. When a relationship becomes the main source of one's identity, there is often disillusionment and the pain of rejection should the partner want to separate. This is why the "Song of Love is a Sad Song". The only way to find a permanent source of a loving connection that can offer a lasting sense of importance and security is by becoming aware of the relationship that you always have with your own Higher Self.

Your Problems Are a Part of Your Identity

You can tell as much about a person if he or she were to describe to you their problems as if they were to tell you about their dreams. Our everyday problems are related to the lenses that our parents put before our eyes and which recreate in our minds the same interpretation of events that they made during their own lifetime. If you write down your most important and pressing problems at this time, you would be revealing important information regarding:

1. The struggle of your parents.
2. The major issues of your childhood.
3. The major challenges you have come to solve this lifetime.

Exercise: Close your eyes and see whether you can bring up pertinent images of the past that still have an emotional impact upon you.

Only a little reflection is needed to help you realize that you have been faced with these problems for as long as you can remember and that they are related to issues of self-image and personal power. Unless the core issue is resolved, your attempts to solve your problems will only result in magnifying and repeating them.

During the period of infancy, emotional resonance is the primary means of communication between parent and child. This works well in the animal kingdom where a mother deer, for example, transmits to her fawn all of the emotions that signal the dangers to be aware of in order to survive. This information is tenaciously held onto by the subconscious mind. In humans, emotionally programmed information is largely fear-based, and so negative emotions underlie most of our attitudes. Even more critical is the fact that your parents did not see the real you! So you are going through life searching for an identity, silently asking everyone you meet, including those who are more lost than you, "Who am I?"

I have counseled many people who were adopted as infants and who were expending considerable energy in an attempt to find their natural parents as if, somehow, this was a way to discover their true identity. The results, when successful, were often disillusioning and an embarrassment to the parent who had concealed the existence of that offspring. More productive would be a continuous effort to make an uplifting connection to your true Mother-Father-God!

How Problems Are Created

There is a process that goes on in the brain that tries to bring a resolution to each experience—a kind of neural completion to obtain a final closure. But any emotional experience that creates a negative impact is almost impossible to "resolve" or to "make okay," without consciously giving it expression. There is something "wrong," or "incomplete," that is threatening to your self-image that remains as a problem that needs to be solved. No closure is possible until the blocked or distorted energy is consciously released. Problems that are held in a secret hiding place in the mind can never be resolved. Part of the resistance to facing the problem is that there is often shame associated with it and the fear that there is no workable solution. The child usually believes that anyone trying to help would only make it worse. Family secrets around incestuous behavior is a common example. The individual needs to know that they are not responsible for the behavior of others and that it takes a higher understanding of the purpose of the experience to come up with a long-term solution.

The problems of today were created in the past. The past is no more than selective memory. We retain most clearly those things to which we attached the most emotion. The solution comes from experiencing fully the linkage between the event and the emotion and breaking the linkage by asking for help to see things differently, or by upgrading our self-image to where the problem no longer exists.

Believing that you have to fix everyone else's problems can also become a major problem in itself. It is natural for young children to want to heal their parents' problems in order to make their own world safe. They feel helpless and worthless when they can't make a difference. Children need to know that they cannot be responsible for the moods or the behavior of their parents.

Then, there are "fix-it" mothers who tend to rush in and try to make everything right by immediately offering solutions or else downgrading the importance of the problem. Their children are likely to grow up feeling inadequate and may resent rather than appreciate their mothers because everyone needs the opportunity to learn how to master life's challenges. The truth is, you cannot help other people by taking their problems away from them. Good therapists help people to solve problems, not by taking them away, but by giving an encouraging push in the right direction that might lead to a discovery of a talent or strength that the person did not know that they possessed.

One woman, with whom I was working, stated she was having a serious problem that didn't have any acceptable solution. She explained that she had been troubled for some time by a daughter who had always been willful and who was now a young adult with a bipolar disorder. However, her daughter refused to take her medications or to listen to any advice and had had to be hospitalized three times in the past year. To make matters worse, the daughter had now become pregnant. She emphasized that this was a "real" and not just an "imagined" problem. I explained that parents should not be blamed for the particular temperament of their children. Neither do we know the life path that her daughter has chosen. For some reason, her daughter had chosen her for her mother. I offered that perhaps the greatest gift that this mother had to offer was not in trying to make her daughter conform to society but to give to her unconditional acceptance as well as her own self as a model. "In any event," I added, "since you feel so strongly about your problem, why don't you bring it to God?" She was ready to try anything. When she sat down to write, the words began to flow and they continued at length with a loving explanation that she had not expected:

Q. God, what can I do for my daughter who is having multiple problems and won't speak to me?

A. A parent is always in a position to be extremely felt or perceived by her child. Your energy could become a new anchor for your daughter. As your daughter sees that it is steady and permanent, she will begin to respond. Your actual energy is the most potent aspect of this encounter. As you begin to relax into confidence and happiness, you will extend a helpful energy to your daughter. Earth beings need to know that everyone's experiences are very valuable to the whole of humanity. Each child foresees the experiences that lay ahead before deciding to undergo the earth journey. The great benefit is not always seen within this lifetime, but blended into the whole it becomes significant. There are homeless individuals who die after a seemingly wasted life, but upon their death bring great benefit to the Higher Self. Parents feel horribly responsible for everything that happens to their children. But their experiences together were mutually agreed upon. It is much like putting on a play, each playing out a different part. Only when the play is over, will all rejoin to appreciate their performances. But you should know that at any age, a positive shift in the energy of the parent will always be sensed by the child who will obtain some measure of healing from this.

This woman, because of the tension she had felt for so many years over her guilt and her anger at her daughter, was also suffering from a variety of arthritic and muscular pains as well as a general feeling of malaise. Again, I suggested she reach out to Higher guidance for an answer.

Q. Why do I have so many physical problems?

A. By your anger at your daughter you are damaging yourself. Your feelings of being inadequate as a mother are upsetting your whole energy balance. You need to realize the limits of your responsibility and the importance of what you do have to offer. Allow Me to guide you in this.

This woman came to realize that she was punishing herself unnecessarily and was trying to control a situation beyond the capacity of her Intellect to obtain the result she wanted. She decided to forgive her daughter and herself as well and to do only what was put before her to handle. The daughter did eventually have a healthy baby girl who was surprisingly precocious. Being the mother of a gifted child changed her daughter's attitude dramatically. She became motivated to be the best mother possible for her child. She began to take her medications, and never needed another hospitalization. In addition she became self-supporting and independent for the first time in her life. The grandchild came to serve as a bridge between mother and daughter.

Why The Same People Keep Having the Same Problems

Problems exist because you have been taught to perceive certain circumstances as unsolvable. When we react mechanically to a problem, like swatting a mosquito, we get only temporary relief at best. A permanent solution requires a conscious decision to make a distinct change in our attitude or mode of coping. Most people are so resistant to change that they will tolerate considerable pain, and even learn to adjust to their discomfort as a tolerable way of life, rather than to risk the unknown, which a change in thinking and behavior might bring. There are a number of reasons for this:

1. They are programmed to "stick" to the problem as their parents did. Fear keeps them hanging onto situations that they should have let go of long ago. Their options tend to be limited to their parents' coping behaviors.

2. The situation requires rethinking, and most children are given admonitions against original thinking. Thus, coping behaviors become restricted to what was permissible during childhood. Unfortunately our society and educational system neglect to teach our young how to examine and to change their thinking patterns.

3. Some people become addicted to their problem. The problem now becomes a familiar way of life, and its solution would leave a void.

4. When a problem is tied to a limited self-image, no amount of good advice" is likely to bring about a significant change in behavior until the roots of the problem are resolved. If you had money problems ten years ago, you probably struggle with money problems today, whether or not you earn a lot more money now. If you had relationship problems ten years ago, you would have similar relationship problems now unless, after a lot of pain, you have learned a new way of relating.

5. Long term decisions become mindsets that make one's reality inflexible and limits the willingness to see new possibilities or to shift behavior. A rigid mindset makes it difficult to comprehend good advice from any source.

6. Many people continue to get into situations that repeatedly trigger outbursts of anger, jealousy, and frustration or fear that only succeeds in reinforcing the unresolved emotions that are held in their brains and the muscles of their body instead of permanently releasing them. The most common unpleasant emotions that are continually reinforced include:

A. Feelings of insecurity, of not being loved, and of not measuring up to some inner or outer standard.

B. A low-grade sense of guilt, blame, or shame that has its roots in early childhood based upon faulty beliefs such as: "I am too needy." "I am responsible for the unhappiness of those about me." "I am deserving of punishment for being selfish or having jealous thoughts". "I am not worthy or deserving of happiness." "I am stupid, wrong, or limited in some way that makes me unlovable."

C. There are residual "knots" of anger held in the various muscles of the body for being invalidated, abused, violated, or treated unfairly. Rage can be repeatedly triggered, long after the initial event, by even a seemingly minor remark by another person that literally shatters the mind and blocks coherent thinking. This is the primary cause of violence in the home.

D. Probably most important are the blockages of energy that were placed upon your spontaneous expression of emotion and behavior. Blocked emotional energy can arrest a person's emotional growth at the age in which it was blocked and erupt explosively in "safe" situations.

Thus an otherwise mature adult in the work place may commonly act like an obstreperous child in the home setting.

E. Victim energy tends to make problems a way of life. Children who has suffered physical and mental abuse will tend to see themselves thereafter as a victim in an uncaring and potentially hostile world.

Many People Need To Be Freed From Victim Energy

There are some people who have a fixed attitude of selfishness, self-righteousness, or an uncommon sense of entitlement. A con artist is one example. There are many other examples in the business world. These attitudes are also prevalent among many dysfunctional youth who refuse to earn money through honest work. However, the vast majority of people have problems that are related to their adoption of "victim energy." People who see themselves as victims will frequently complain, try to make other people into victims, become depressed and feel sorry for themselves, are prone to emotional outbursts, often become verbally abusive and may even resort to self-righteous violence. Young men, who have low self-esteem and a life-long pattern of feeling victimized, perpetrate the majority of senseless crimes in this country. For most people, however, victim energy leads to a general sense of helplessness and a lackluster life. Many well-meaning people who are not successful and are dissatisfied with their lives need to free themselves from victim energy before they can accomplish anything of significance. They need to learn the following two rules regarding victim energy:

1. What you complain about today you will undoubtedly complain about tomorrow.
2. No amount of nagging has ever brought about a permanent positive change in the behavior of another person.

Do not be wavered by the demands of others who will try to make you feel uncomfortable and guilty. The world imposes a misconception of responsibility that makes it related to taking on more weight, duty, and sacrifice to fulfill the needs of others. Responsibility means taking charge of your own energy and utilizing it in the way that best suits you. You are not being selfish when you are taking care of yourself. This is the only way to receive more energy and joy to share with others. Remember the advice of the airline stewardess as the airplane is ready to take off: "If there is a problem, put your own oxygen mask on first—even before your own child."

Your problem might be stated to God as a grievance, with a request for relief. Because you cannot see the whole picture, there is the need for patience and perseverance. So do not judge the nature of the help you receive in the short term, but trust in the final outcome. The solution often seems like a miracle because it involves a major shift in your own self-perception first, which then leads to a change in your outer circumstances. The worst decision of all is to go into inner bitterness or self-destructive rebellion against the world.

Jim's Lesson About Mindset

Mindset is one of the most difficult things to change once it has been firmly established. Even reaching a point of willingness to change it is a major accomplishment. Jim had held onto a mindset despite the pleading of his wife and the advice of friends, until it almost killed him.

Jim ran a glass shop with a partner who was not carrying his share of the load. His work schedule exacted a heavy toll upon his body but he was determined to prove that he could succeed in business. He also could see no alternatives for making a living. He continued for almost thirteen years, dreading to wake up each morning to go to work. He was in the wrong setting with the wrong partner. He prayed every day to make his business work when it was his circumstances that needed to change. But his self-image was tied to it and he could not see any options. The more painful it became, the more he turned to liquor to numb it. His health deteriorated until it became critical that he be placed on medical disability for one year. His partner elected to take over the business and shortly afterward this partner died of a heat attack. While recuperating, Jim realized that he never wanted to return to work as a glazier again.

However, he discovered he had many talents that could be used to do jobs requiring specialized handiwork for private individuals. His business grew by word of mouth until he was making more than the net salary he was making before, and with infinitely more enjoyment.

Jim had many talents as a superb craftsman and had a gift for understanding and fixing mechanical things, including those that he had never worked on before. He also had a knack for noting quality. For example, he accompanied a friend, who was a musician, to buy a new piano. He noted differences in the construction of different models. His friend was able to make a decision based upon a multiple of elements that Jim was able to point out to him.

Jim began to ask for a greater expansion of conscious awareness and understanding and one day he came to me to eagerly share what he had come to learn over the past year:

Happiness is not something that is difficult or impossible to achieve but, for some reason, I never even considered happiness as an attainable goal. Everything depends upon mindset and self-image. If your life isn't working you have to pray for help in changing your mindset that keeps you holding onto the unworkable situation. The more difficult the situation the harder I tried. My situation was something like playing my favorite game of scrabble. You might have a rack that has a great word on it. If you become stuck, you can only see that one word. You could force it, but it doesn't give you many points. You might complain that there may not be a good place to put it. If you will give up your insistence upon maintaining that word and look at the letters themselves, and the possibility for rearranging them, you may find a word in which you set several letters aside but score a greater number of points. You have to go to a different level of awareness than our educational system touches upon. It doesn't answer the deeper questions. It doesn't bring awareness to how powerful the mind is as a tool to attract what you want and to create the reality you desire.

The little me and big Me are seamless. If I trust only my own ingenuity, I'm stuck. I had seen and evaluated things in a certain way that formulated a skewed belief system. The initial step may be painful and difficult because it involves confusion and a change of identity. You don't know your real value and therefore the situation seems to have no answers. Your value does not lie in your work as a businessman but who you are as a Being.

I sat back and took the above notes verbatim as Jim enthusiastically shared with me what he had learned the past year and how his mindset had put him into an impossible situation. When patients begin to lecture to me like this, I know that they finally "got it."

Giving Up Problem Habits

There are dozens of books on the shelves of every bookstore that explain how to do things right. The ones you like the best are usually those that tell you what you already know. That is your biggest problem. You can't make yourself do what you already know you should be doing. That is the continuing source of your helplessness, defensiveness and guilt. You might decide, as many people do, to put your life in the hands of someone else. Then you become filled with anger and resentment because they are so unqualified to meet your expectations. Or, like the vast majority, you may seek comfort in bodily pleasures or by going unconscious in front of a television set or else by engaging frenetically in some repetitive activity, much like a hamster turning a wheel. The urge to go unconscious has fed billions of dollars into pharmaceutical houses that are willing to oblige.

A confused mind cannot heal itself. It is all right to go to therapists or to teachers who can bring you to their own level of understanding. However, there is a level of teaching that is constantly attempting to make contact with you, but can't get through your shell of fear, defensiveness, stubbornness, righteousness, and all the defenses you have put up against a world that you see as uncaring, competitive, demanding and, sometimes, insane. Your thinking pattern has become an addiction that can be more difficult to give up than an alcohol or drug addiction because it contains your self-identity.

Upsets Fill Your Head With Problems

Everyone has their own list of upsets running through their head which makes life stressful and that are difficult to stop without asking for help from a higher Source. These play and replay like a looped tape just below the level of consciousness. They represent a learned thinking pattern that has been physiologically ingrained in our brains in early childhood. Our close relationships are contaminated by the energy of these upsets that often has nothing to do with the given situation. They cannot be changed by attacking them directly, but by making affirmations of truth that gradually set up new, positive neurological pathways. Spiritual help is needed as well, because these upsets have the power of addictions. They impact your personality and self-concept.

You can walk downtown on a busy street and see people struggling to untangle their thoughts. They talk to themselves with troubled faces, hardly noticing their surroundings. Upsets form a cloud in our preconscious mind that covers our heads and affects our perceptions of the moment. They invariably instill the negative emotions of resentment, worry, indignation, frustration, or guilt that we often turn upon ourselves as well. This is sometimes experenced as a heavy pressure on either side of the head, and predisposes us to tension headaches. Each person has their own specific pattern that includes any or all of the following:

1. Fear or anger over other's critical judgments (especially by family members).
2. Worry about the future or the health of those you care about.
3. Regrets about the past and remorse over wasted opportunities.
4. Guilt for not performing up to self-expectations and not completing all the things you have to do.
5. Outrage at the indifference or incompetence of those you have depended upon.
6. Expectations of being cheated, used, or being taken advantage of.
7. Self reproach because of a failure to confront someone who deserved it.
8. Nursing old grievances, including not being appreciated.
9. Having responsibilities, financial or otherwise, that create a feeling of insecurity or lack.
10. Resentments toward others whom you blame for your stressful living situation and problematic events in your life.

What is generally not recognized is that these upsets constitute an habitual state of mind that is compulsively reproduced by releasing anger, expressing blame, complaining, or making others feel guilty. It is a massive deterrent against being free to clearly and openly experience the present. These thoughts, if reinforced by the wrong companions, can develop into depressive moods, paranoia, or the justification for violence.

That is why your choice of friends is very important, as well as the need to constantly monitor your thoughts. But, remember that you need Higher help to permanently change them.

Thinking worrisome thoughts is a habit pattern that is learned in childhood, and which sustains and limits your self-image. We all have unlimited power to improve our moods by changing our thoughts. All it requires is a sincere willingness to do so. One of the most important realizations that comes from doing inner work is that your feelings in the moment, including your anger, anxiety, and worries are largely reruns of the past. These thoughts are your constant companions from which you cannot escape without conscious effort and help. We have become addicted to thinking patterns, attitudes, habits, and a way of life that does not really serve us. When a little child plays with a spool of yarn, it will become entangled to the point where it will be impossible for the child to untangle it by himself. His efforts will only create tighter knots. But no harm has been done. He calls in mommy who can untangle it quite easily. Similarly our thoughts have become so entangled that we cannot escape from them without help from a Higher Source.

The Orange-Lemon Mind trip

If you doubt the power of your thoughts read the following exercise and then repeat it with your eyes closed:

You are taking a long hike through a scenic park. It is a very hot day and you neglected to bring a supply of water. After a few hours you find yourself becoming increasingly thirsty and begin to look for an exit where you might be able to find some water. Finally, you find a path that leads to the street of a small city area. You see a grocery store on the corner of the street and eagerly head for it in the hope of finding something to quench your thirst. As you enter you see a neat stack of large oranges. The grocery man approaches you and remarks: "We received this shipment of juicy oranges just today. Try one and you will want to buy a dozen of them." You place an orange in the palm of your hand and peel back the skin. Then you stick your finger into the center and pull free a piece of the pulp. You put it into your mouth and chew down, feeling its sweet juice pour down your dry throat.

As you are enjoying this orange, the grocer adds that he also received a large shipment of sour lemons. He takes one of the lemons and places it on the chopping block to offer you a piece. You take the slice of lemon into your mouth and suck hard on it. What does it taste like?

Can you feel the difference between sucking on the orange and sucking on the lemon? There are undoubtedly concomitant physiological changes in your body as well, which might be measured with the proper instruments. There are some people who go through life mentally sucking on lemons. You can tell this by their faces and their demeanor. Why not envision something sweet that brings a smile to your face?

The Nature and Proper Function of the Intellect

Most of today's stress, as the world becomes more complex, is due to using the Intellect in ways in which it was not meant to function. The Intellect's job is to integrate and synthesize the input from the five senses in order to orient an individual to the environment. It then considers and makes statements that integrates or make sense of the environment without having to repeatedly re-evaluate old patterns over and over. The Intellect makes decisions based upon a belief system that is developed in early childhood and that now operates like the default settings in a computer.

This belief system about the world, and who you are in this world, develops primarily from :

> 1. The belief system of parents and authority figures in early childhood.

> 2. Conclusions drawn about the world from early experiences and during the "latency years" up

until puberty. These remain largely unchanged into adult life, especially when a strong emotional component is attached to them. These beliefs about yourself and the world are influenced by both peer pressure and outside authority. There is a tendency   to conform your beliefs to those who are important to you out of a fear of upsetting the balance. The Intellect defines the comfort zone, the belief system that offers the most safety, and tries to keep you there.

The newborn infant is faced with the task of making sense of a psychedelic world that has no meaning. During infancy, it functions primarily from the emotional center, linking a specific energy to each event in order to gain later recognition and predictability to its environment. In doing this, the child primarily reaches out to its mother to create emotional connections to each situation that resonate closely with hers.

The development of a vocabulary permits the emerging Intellect to put basic premises into words that function as default settings that color all future conclusions and judgments regarding all new experiences. The greater the emotion attached to a premise, the more power it holds over all future impressions of reality.

The Intellect is the rational or reasoning part of the mind, but in man it reasons irrationally because its roots were contaminated by the fear of the ego that enforced basic premises that say, "I am an isolated body." "I am vulnerable and must defend myself from the dangerous world that I perceive." "I must also defend myself against pain by curtailing my deepest yearnings and desires and, especially, not to love because it will be turned against me." When the Intellect adopts this limited concept of self, its conclusions can only lead to a sense of aloneness, an inner malaise, a sense of alienation and a deadening of life. And this, in turn, results in convoluting the aim of life into that of controlling or dominating the outer world. Even then the self has little value. This can be attested to by the fact that it can be greatly elevated by the attainment of a handsome salary, a new car, or a large house. We have arrived at the height of irrationality when the worth of the immortal Soul is judged by the accumulation of mortal things. The use of drugs, especially by our youth, is symptomatic of a desperate attempt to escape, like a caged bird, from this narrow concept of life.

Our culture does not address the one question we should be asking, "What is the meaning of my existence?" Only the inward life can find communion with the answer. For where better than within oneself can man find the meaning of his own existence—the "It" that was there before the ego, and before the ego became distracted and began directing the Intellect to look in the opposite direction.

The beginning step to opening new doors in any area of your life is to quiet the boisterous thinking mechanism, even though you may have been taught that the opposite is the more useful way to succeed. The thinking mechanism is the means by which the brain synthesizes the input from the five senses as well as the emotional charge attached to each. It is not the thinking mechanism's place to find solutions. Its place is to invite or direct impulses of thought or energy. To open the door to higher, intuitive knowing involves a shift to a different level of energy, not a door on the same level. This can be done with a spirit of discovery. You must quiet the thinking area, and hold only the feeling of intent to open the door. This lowers resistance (as in an electrical system), and opens a space for higher spiritual energy to enter. The thinking area must also be attentive and receptive to the energy invited. Then it is possible to experience a higher level of oneself. With this comes a sense of inner satisfaction, flow, and a compatibility that brings the desire to spread this energy outward to one's life.

The earth dimension is intended to be one of exploration and creation; an adventure in which the energy of an individual feels separate and yet a part of everything. It offers the potential experience of power, pleasure, mastery, and new experiences. Questions are continually arising which compel answers that move us into new directions. We tend to lose sight of our own truth because of external influences. Conventional educational systems impose the incorrect use of consciousness and serve to split the Intellect from the Inner Self. This results in self-invalidation, doubt, and inner conflict. We must learn to know our Inner Self as the loving resource it truly is, and a true companion to the inner child.

The result of mental pursuing of meaning is draining. "How can there be well-being in the midst of what is so wrong?" A simple beginning to free yourself from the past is to ask, "What if everything was really okay?" "How then would each event appear?" Learn to look for an important, mind-enhancing lesson in each event. You will first have to see it and approach it in a new way. The most critically important moment is the energy generated later, rather than at the time of the incident itself. Thus, even tragic events are a treasure chest of growth material. Begin to ask questions: "What is it I must experience, discover, learn?" See it with excitement. Focus on the expectations of positive experiences. Speak positively to the turbulent moments. Ask: "What was there for me to see?"

Our brains cannot comprehend the complex trajectories of energy resulting from our daily interactions. Events of great significance are arranged for us because of the ultimate benefit derived. The purpose may be beyond our present comprehension. There is much more to the story than you can understand from this level. But when a person feels most lost or frustrated the opportunity for positive change is greatest.

Want is a launching pad to enormous benefit. The energy of frustration and discouragement can become the energy that overcomes inertia to launch oneself into a new arena. Closed doors are not locked doors. Learn to shift energy from despair to anticipation. Make affirmations: "I have every right to experience a state of comfort and self-acceptance."

Be aware when you feel anxious, worried, and caught up in reruns of the past. The inner dialogue keeps you company, but also keeps you stuck in the past as you review one angry incident after another. Stop it!! It is all archeology, and you are still living there. Everyone has a voice in their head telling them what to do and what people think. It is full of anger and anxiety. It fluctuates between hope and despair.

Most people do not know what to ask for or what they really want. They primarily know what they don't want, which is a problem because that's what they've got. This is not only due to a lack of emphasis in our educational system on teaching how to think for yourself, how to know what you really want, and how to make decisions to get what you want—but even more serious—the nature of our currect system of education may actually create a mental block against this type of original thinking! We have been told what to think. Thus, most people cannot think, plan or make decisions. Most arguments between husband and wife arise because neither knows how to make fruitful decisions, and each blames the other for allowing problems to come up as the result of their own inadequacies.

Even many musical and mathematical geniuses are unable to make simple decisions around the basic running of their lives.

Attaining academic honors or becoming a PhD or MD has nothing to do with making life decisions. Be aware of how the Intellect seeks comfort in busyness and repetitious activities. Your Intellect is incapable of thinking a new thought or coming up with a new, creative idea or invention. These only occur through intuition, the result of quiet attunement to answers coming from a Higher level. It is a fact that many of our well-known inventions or discoveries occurred to the inventor in a dream. Examples include the sewing machine needle, the Xerox machine, and the structure of the benzene molecule. It was primarily through the use of intuition that I was able to devise and publish (with a foreword by Garry Kasparov) an innovative system of chess that can defeat today's best chess computer programs.

The conscious Intellect is only a speck in the ocean of emotion. The more we try to use our Intellects as the only thing running our life, the more our life becomes a comico-tragic television sitcom in which each character sees problems where there are none, and then escalates the condition or the situation in an attempt to solve their self-created problems. The ego differs from the Intellect in that the ego represents a thought form of who you are. The Intellect incorporates this into its decision-making functions. In most humans the ego is fear-based. This is a learned and not an inherent quality of the ego.

Letting Go of Problems

Realize that the way you feel this very moment has everything to do with what you are telling yourself right now:

> What you should be doing now instead of sitting here.
> What you should have done differently in the past.
> What you need to do in the future.
> Concern about the things that people think about you.
> Problems you need to solve in your relationships.
> Obsession with bodily functions
> Comparing your money, intelligence, influence, likableness and power with others you label as friends, colleagues, or peers.

Many people block the busy thoughts going on in their heads by constant external stimulation. They read while they eat. They read when they go to the bathroom. They read while they run on the treadmill at the gym. They put on the television set when they are alone and, often, even with family. They have no time because they go through it unconsciously. They cannot remember where they left something ten minutes ago. Their Intellect is always replaying the past and cannot find a comfort zone where everything is in its proper place.

A trusting sense of detachment could do wonders to your level of anxiety and stress. This means cultivating the habit of looking at ongoing problems as merely situations you are going through.

Your identification with what is happening and your need to change it is what causes problems. Learn to look at life without feeling so personally involved, much the way that you watch your favorite television program The central character usually perceives a relatively minor relationship problem as much worse than it is, and then magnifies it with aggressive behavior. The resulting upset and loud arguments are accompanied with canned laughter.

Who are the heroes of our movies? They are men who act with conviction and without fear. Unfortunately they convey that their physical prowess and hyperawareness are necessary to keep them fearless. They are still continuously surrounded by enemies and are motivated by revenge. In most stories the hero or heroine appears to effectively put an end to their problems by a display of violence.   This is not the message that alleviates fear in people. In the media, the weak and helpless are still victims, and suffering comes to those who are the most innocent. The television series, "Touched by an Angel", is the only program I can now find on television where love is used as the way to solve a major problem.

Try to envision the manner in which love, rather than intimidation, could solve problems. Situations are something to be handled as a vehicle for growth and not with fear or anger which festers until violence appears to be the only solution. Trust the power that you have within you to change a specific situation or person that is bothering you and creating a problem. by sending the love that is needed to change the situation.

But how will our children learn to solve problems this way when our society has not learned it.

God will not force you to open up your heart. That is something you must decide to do. If you have difficulty doing it, that is because your heart does not believe you. Now you can ask for the understanding and the feeling of self-love that will allow you to open your heart. Reflect upon how all of your problems of the past could have been healed by the exchange of love by all concerned. But if the others cannot do it, the problem remains theirs, and not yours. Believe that you do have enough time to complete what needs to be completed. Learn the secret of "making haste slowly." Time is very subjective. The lack of time or money is never the original cause of any of your problems.

How to Ask for Help

First you have to decide whether you really want help. When people talk about their problems with each other, sometimes they want sympathy or validation of how they are currently coping with their problems, but they are rarely asking for an answer that will force them to radically change their behavior. There are three types of people who come to you with problems.

1. The complainers who make the rounds each day of every friend willing to listen to their problems. Each friend gives his or her differing opinion as to what should be done, but the problem never changes. All the complainers want is confirmation that they are innocent victims deserving of sympathy.

2. The complaint collectors who willingly listen empathetically. This may provide them with a social function that is often expanded into the role of the person who "knows all the dirt" and is willing to spread it. Even some therapists fall into the trap of becoming paid complaint collectors, seeing the same patients for years around the same problems without a solution in sight.

3. Those who do not want to play this game. If you want to discourage want-to-be friends from dumping the same complaints on you each time you meet, you can discourage them by forcing them out of victim energy with the following questions: "What are you going to do differently in the future?" "What is your role in perpetuating this problem?" "What is your need for this problem?" Chronic complainers learn quickly who are receptive to merely collecting their complaints and who are not. Those who do not want to play either side of this game and who genuinely want answers are in a position to receive help.

Following Are the Steps to Ask for Help:

1. Express openly the fear, anxiety, or problem you are facing. Writing to God can be especially helpful.

2. State what is wanted: "I want to handle this successfully and with comfort." "I want to feel good about this." "I want to feel good more than I want to feel angry."

3. Then, leave it alone, while trusting that the answer will be forthcoming. The answer will be specifically designed for what the asker needs and can use. The final answer does not depend upon your knowing but your listening.

4. Expect that real changes will occur by the act of placing your attention upon it. This is not merely psychological. Quantum physicists have noted for some time that their belief and expectations actually have an effect upon what they are observing.

5. When you bring your problem to God, expect an answer.

A New Approach to Old Problems

Once a situation is perceived as a problem you can no longer solve it by yourself. This overloads the intellectual center, which is not meant to solve problems. The Intellect is primarily a receiver and synthesizer of the five senses, colored by the ego's sense of self. Our society's drive to overload the Intellect today by forcing it to memorize large amounts of rote information in order to make complex decisions is largely due to a denial of a Higher Center of knowing. This has resulted in an increase in stress and depression in even young children today because they do not know that they have a Higher Center for problem-solving.

The answer to a problem is often found in a clear definition of the problem itself. Much of psychotherapy is involved in helping to clearly define the problem, and then listening carefully in order to understand the perspective from which the problem has been created. As stated earlier, a problem is a distinctly personal experience. It consists of a perception coupled with an attitude that results in a feeling of upset or discomfort. We might define a problem as a situation involving uncertainty or difficulty that requires a decision. If the decision comes easily, then there's no problem. Thus, a problem can only be defined by the person who experiences it. A different person, seeing the situation from a different perspective, may not see a major problem in the situation, and may offer all kinds of good advice that cannot be acted upon because the basic core of the problem, which lies within the self-image of the other person, remains unchanged.

The cure of a perceived problem does not always require a magical solution, but rather a restatement of the problem: "Right now I believe that. . . , however, I am convinced that there is another way of seeing things." The statements holding the situation in an unsolvable position can be changed at several points if one is willing to deal with the discomfort of change. It requires a giving up on the old and familiar way of judging things. It is especially uncomfortable when intuitive impulses suggest doing something while another part is afraid of letting go of the tangible circumstances. It is something like the game of pick-up sticks. There is the fear that the shifting of any one piece can cause the whole pile to collapse.

Steps to Freeing Yourself From Problems

1. Define the structure of the problem. What is your experience of it?

2. How did you create it? (What pattern of behavior in you set it up?) When did you first learn this behavior?

3. What is your need for it? What void does it fill? Does the experience bond you to a parent who often felt the same way during your childhood?

4. What unawareness in you perpetuates it? Be honest in your recognition that it is not entirely new.

5. Envision the experience of rising above it. Is this consistent with your self-image? What new problem might this bring up if you rise above it?

6. Are you willing to see the problem as a teacher? What weakness in you must be strengthened?

After you have honestly considered the above, ask God to add to your awareness of it. The emotional component must be strongly experienced before you can detach it from your Intellect. Then ask for God's help to move on. Lessons learned do not have to be repeated.

6

The Nature of Crises

Common situations that require some form of practical intervention, if too long ignored or improperly handled, can grow into problems. Problems, as previously described, tend to persist and may become accepted as a normal way of life. However, some problems that are indefinitely denied or ignored can result in a crisis such as a life-threatening disease or a situation involving violence or a major loss of life or property. A crisis differs from a problem in that it represents a major catastrophic event that creates an undeniable shift in how a person sees and copes with life thereafter.

Many crises, however, are not merely the result of situations that were mishandled. There are some crises that seem to hit you from out of nowhere. Your life may seem to be going along relatively predictably when, like suddenly smashing into a stone wall, you are forced into a unexpected and dramatic change in direction. Crises create a shock effect that threatens the stability of everything that previously held together your self-concept, and your physical reality. Depending upon how they are subsequently handled, they can lead either to a new level of growth or to a permanent state of debilitation.

The Chinese word for "crisis" also means "opportunity." It is not uncommon to hear of people who have reported a spontaneous spiritual transformation following a cataclysmic turn of fortune that leaves them stripped of all of their previous resources. Unfortunately, it is more common without the proper support, to see one's life direction following a major crisis move in the direction of some form of permanent disability, drug use, withdrawal from social contacts, and even suicide. As an example, consider that you had been the captain of the Titanic and had survived. How might that event have affected the remainder of your life?

Major life crises can leave a lasting effect upon self-concept. Since the 1970's, when the term Post Traumatic Stress Disorder (PTSD) was introduced into the psychiatric literature, there has become an increasing awareness of the number of people who suffer from some degree of this disorder and that it can date back to early childhood trauma.

Having dealt with a large variety of crises during my professional career, I have found it useful to define the nature of a particular crisis into one of three distinct categories, all of which have to do with a devastating dissolution of the ego and, with this, a loss of an acceptable sense of an intact self.

The Three Categories of Crises

1. Catastrophic Loss.

A catastrophic loss may be the loss of a spouse, close relative, a friend, a major body part, the uprooting from cherished surroundings, or the sudden loss of significant wealth. The identity had become so attached with these sources of fulfillment that a painful void is felt in the person's entire psyche by this loss. Clinically, the symptoms are manifested as depression and grief. There is an unwillingness to accept the loss and a strong desire to die rather than to go on. The person gradually reintegrates his or her identity by going through the process of mourning. Painful gut-wrenching emotion comes in waves that overwhelm rational thinking and even the will to live. The process of mourning has its stages of denial, guilt, anxiety and panic, depression, anger, and reaching out to others analogus to the process of dying as has been well described by Elizabeth Kubler-Ross and others.

The failure to go through a proper mourning process may lead to a variety of lasting symptoms as described by Lindemann in his classical work following the Oak Grove nightclub fire in Boston in 1953. I was a senior in college and living in Boston at the time, and was intrigued by the newspaper coverage about his findings following his interviews with survivors. He later published the residual deficits that he noted in many of these survivors that included: rigidity of personality, chronic depression, self-destructive behavior, taking upon oneself the traits of the dead person, and lifelong guilt.   Of interest he concluded that grief from the loss of a child is the most difficult to overcome.

2. Massive Ego Insult or Shock That Results In a Loss of Sense of Self.

The person has been put into a situation of either committing atrocities or becoming a victim of a reprehensible act.. Bruno Bettleheim and Viktor Frankl are two psychiatrists who have written extensively about their own experiences of depersonalization and identity confusion in concentration camps. (Bruno Bettleheim, based upon his own painful feelings, wrongly assumed that similar experiences lay behind the cause of childhood autism.)

Franz Fanon, in his book, Wretched of the Earth (1965), describes atrocities committed by both sides in the French-Algerian War, and gives examples of emotional breakdown following the accidental or unthinking performance of acts that are totally irreconcilable with that person's self-image. This predicated the causalities from Post Traumatic Stress Syndrome that we were later to be seen in veterans of the Vietnam War. I have recently been made aware of the statistic that as many veterans of the Vietnam War ultimately committed suicide as were killed in combat.

The traumatic incident evokes extreme emotions of fear, cowardice, or sadistic impulses that fragment the identity structure and evoke a compelling desire to escape from one's own self-image, feelings and thoughts. The identity becomes so bound to the event in memory that there may be a strong disgust or alienation from oneself. Untreated, we see a number of social problems arising out of this syndrome, including multiple personalities, drug abuse, and self-destructive behaviors including crimes of violence to attract punishment. Chronic psychosomatic complaints are common in those who have been callously violated, along with an emotional regression to a constant feeling of helplessness. The more recent psychiatric literature is now documenting the lasting effects of severe mental or physical abuse in childhood to lasting problems in later life. Recent, highly publicised, examples are that of young male adults who were sexually molested by authority figures as children, and who later commited sucide.

3. Ego Failure

A shattering of one's self-image can result from a failed responsibility that eventually leads to serious consequences. It can range from the failure of a marriage to the loss of a ship by its captain. There is usually an associated strong feeling of disbelief or panic and an inner loss of trust in one's future ability to cope. This can lead to social withdrawal or else into a child-like regression of helplessness and a reaching out for consolation. It may also result in wildly paranoid outbursts in which blame is projected upon others. In the death of a child from a drug overdose or from neglect, it can lead to chronic depression from unrelenting guilt. Many of these individuals may remain a high risk for suicide, even after many years, especially when others were seriously harmed or died as a result of their perceived failure. One example is, the captain of the heavy cruiser, Indianapolis, which was torpedoed in shark infested waters in the South Pacific during WWII. Over half of his crew who were in life jackets or hanging onto the side of lifeboats were attacked and eaten by sharks during the long night. He survived, but was so haunted by this memory that he committed suicide some twenty years later.

In each of these categories of crises that engender either extreme grief, shock, or panic the use of an experienced therapist would be very helpful in providing a supportive environment to assist recall and to offer a place of safety to release the long held emotions around a particular traumatic incident. There are a number of techniques and tools now used for reawakening repressed memories and to desensitize or to resolve past trauma on a cognitive and emotional level. In my experience, all of these techniques have their usefulness, but rarely have I witnessed a complete healing or complete release without the intervention of an intrinsic spiritual belief that attributes the incident, for whatever purpose, to the design of a Higher Power.

Finding a spiritual purpose to the trauma and knowing that whatever pain was experienced was not wasted is essential to a final resolution, and is the only way to reach enough understanding to offer and to accept genuine forgiveness. The

Core Self can never be damaged in any way. Once this is clearly accepted, the past can be released as if it were no more than the memory of a dream and a new self can rise out of the ashes of the old. Thus the presence of a strong spiritual belief is essential to attaining a lasting resolution in each of these categories of crises. Unfortunately, without openness to spiritual help, the direction is more likely to be one toward some form of permanent disability, drug use, withdrawal from social contacts, and even suicide. Such was the fate of many veterans of the Vietnam War.

Cathy's Grief Process

Cathy was grieving over her husband's death in a private plane crash. Her entire life revolved around him. He made all of their life decisions. She was constantly beside him, helping him with his business. They had three children who were now young adults and had already left home. She was so devastated by the loss that she found it hard to get out of bed each day and had no motivation to do anything for five years prior to her coming to see me. A major problem was her fear of going to sleep each night, which consequently left her fatigued throughout the day. She expressed guilt for not being there with him as well as anger toward God for letting it happen. "I'm all alone." "I can't cope." "He was everything to me." "Is God punishing me?" "I don't care what His reason might have been. I will never accept it." "I'll never be happy again." "My heart is sad and in pain."

Cathy had already undergone conventional grief counseling without much relief. After several sessions, I suggested that since she had brought up the word "God" fairly frequently that she vent her anger directly at God. Even if she accepted the possibility that there are no accidents and that there was a special purpose in her experiencing this crisis, she could not be expected to accept it at this stage when all she felt was devastation. The following are excerpts from several sessions in which she released considerable emotion. She then tried some simple meditative practices to quiet her mind so that she could sleep.

Q. God, I have no faith but I still have fight. I won't give up. My Soul will survive. I have faith but no trust anymore. Do I believe? Sometimes I feel like I do. Are You on my side? What did I do to deserve all the punishment you are throwing at me? Take it back. I want to be happy. I'm afraid to be happy because you will take it away.

A. Dear Cathy, your greatest fear is being afraid; but afraid of what? You have been through the worst of it. You have yet to discover your true strength.

Q. How do I avoid being hurt again?

A. By trusting yourself, God, and the people that are now being drawn to you. Have more faith in yourself to persevere. Your connection to your husband is not lost.

He is trying to help from the other side. He is going to see a positive part in you that he did not see before.

Q. God, why do I have so much trouble meditating; having a silent mind? I seem to hang on for dear life.

A: Your mind thinks you have to do everything right and it is too much of a burden on your Intellect. Take baby steps. Start with just noticing your breath. See the task as making friends with your breath. In a sense you are trying to make friends with Me. When you try to communicate with Me, you feel that you are approaching a big power outside of yourself and you are frightened and afraid to do it wrong. Take small steps. Start with being a baby and progress at your own pace. We are building a relationship.

Q. *Dear God, I need your help. I keep straying from my intention of focusing on You and seeing with Your eyes and hearing with Your ears. Please help me to help myself. What should I do?*

A. It's not about doing. It's about taking time to allow, to quiet down, to become centered, and to wait. Meditating is an allowing practice.

Q. How can I take control of my life and do what I intend?

A: You allow through deep intentions the shift in desire. The desire and the pleasure of stillness must build. It is an acquired taste.

Q. God, why is it so difficult to get myself organized?

A. You have your possessions in boxes, in storage, and scattered all about the house without spending quality time bringing everything together. It is like the state of your mind, scattered and without focus at this time. Structuring your environment will help to structure your mind. It will be the sign of demonstrating that you are beginning to care again.

Q. My eyes are so tired they hurt, but I can't go to sleep at night.

A. Your stream of negative thinking creates knots in your head. Trust God to unravel the knots and to run the world while you are sleeping.

Q. A woman in a man's world without a man is helpless.

A. You will learn to teach other women that they are equal to men, and not to be afraid of them.

Q. I feel like I have nothing to hold onto anymore. I'm afraid I'm pushing people away on purpose because I don't want them to like me. I want them to hate me.

A. You have some thing to hold onto that can never be taken away.

Q. All those people who lost loved ones in the New York Trade Center are going through what I'm going through, like there's nothing left.

A. You cannot see the greater picture, but you can begin to make the greater connection.

Following the above sequence, Cathy commented to me: "I don't understand the answers I'm getting, but somehow I feel better afterwards."

Cathy needed to learn her own worth and value independentl from anyone else. She needed to learn to grow by extending herself into the world. Gradually she was encouraged to take courses to become a paralegal. This proved to help her immensely in resolving legal issues around the sale of her husband's business. She also volunteered as a member of a non-profit organization that helps underprivileged children. She began making a stronger connection to her own children and especially to her granddaughter who is very intelligent and attractive but self-conscious about having a severe hearing impairment from birth.

She began meeting other women with similar problems around loss and found words to comfort them. She began to realize that despite the fact that she was one of ten children, she had her own uniqueness as a member of her family. She began reading books, both fiction and non-fiction – whatever she was drawn to when she entered a bookstore. She found that she was a much stronger woman than she had previously envisioned. She claims that she now often feels the encouraging presence of her deceased husband supporting her from the other side. A love story need not end with the death of a partner. She is able to accept that he had completed his mission in giving her a sense of value, but left so that she would learn that her worth was not dependent on just one human being.

Cathy's world is continually expanding. Most important she has now become an especially loving being and a very desirable woman who has no shortage of serious, well-educated men who vie for her company.

David's Answers

David was suffering from a severe post-traumatic stress disorder as the result of a very uncomfortable work environment in a large corporation where he had been a very conscientious and well-liked worker for the past twenty-five years. But, with major changes and technological upgrading, the environment had suddenly changed dramatically and his new supervisors treated him with hostility and disrespect. His symptoms progressed, over the past two years, into a major depression with panic attacks, so that he was forced to go on medical disability. He suffered from nightmares and became so fearful that he was unable to do the normal tasks around the house that he was accustomed to do in the past. Adding to his stress were the reports of his Worker's Compensation physician who accused him of malingering. He needed some kind of support or outlet between his sessions with me to bind his anxiety. The exercise of writing to God seemed ideal. He was surprised by the results of his initial attempt:

Q. Dear Jesus, please tell me what is happening to me. Will I ever feel well again?

A. Dear David, be assured that all will work out well in the end. There are those who love you and will support you. You have been created as a beautiful and wonderful person and I love you more than you know. Your sensitivity has caused you great distress. With time, care, patience, and the help of others you will not only be well but you will be better than before.

Q. When you said I would be well again, what just exactly did you mean?

A. Dear David, your idea of well and my idea of well differ quite a bit. I told you that in time with the help of those who love you, that you would indeed be well. Well is what I make you to be for My purpose not yours. I am not going to make you well as you imagine it to be. If that were so you would return to your former way of living, thinking, and values. That is not what I have in store for you. With respect to your illness, you will always have this problem and it will always limit you. But it will not limit Me. You may recall, in the Bible, how My servant, Paul, was afflicted with a physical condition that limited him. Though he asked me three times, I did not remove this condition. It was placed there by Me so that he would better be able to serve Me and my purpose. So it is with you. Your life has changed forever, but it doesn't mean it is over. It will now be different and, I fully expect you to eventually think, better.

Q. Dear Jesus, why did the medications not help me?

A. The medications would only have allowed you to return to the former way in which you were working and living. In the long run they would not have helped you to discover the life changes that are necessary to make your life more complete and fulfilling. It is time for you to go into a new direction and a new future. The best is yet to come.

Q. Dear Jesus, I just found out last night that my stepfather has prostate cancer. Will he survive the cancer?

A. Dear David, this is not for you to know. What I do want you to know is that this will be a very difficult time for both him and your mother. I want you to be very close to them during this time. Be with them. Love them. Help them. Be still and quiet and know what I have in store for them and how I plan to use you to help them.

Q. Higher Self, I feel like I have a lot of flaws. I'm not good on my feet when the pressure is on and I know it. So how can I feel confident knowing this in the back of my mind? What can I do about it?

A. Dear David, everybody has flaws. Everybody makes mistakes. The problem is that you are thinking about your flaws which draws energy to them and this happens the most when you are under pressure and most vulnerable. You need to focus on the task at hand and trust that you will find a way to get it done.

Q. *Can I turn to You for help when I'm feeling pressure?*

A. You can ask My advice any time. The answers are always there. In fact, you know what the answers are. But I can help you remind yourself of what the answers are.

Q. Dear Jesus, please help me see my life before me. What can I do to help my inner child not to feel so uptight and feel more relaxed?

A. Stay calm. Look to Me for guidance. Feel me in your self. Quiet yourself by hearing Me in your heart. You will slowly feel at ease with My presence in your Soul. I will guide you through your obstacles if you are willing to let Me. Walk with Me and see that I can take care of you and I will as you are My child and I love you and will protect you.

Q. Dear Jesus, why do I want to turn to Buddha instead of You?

A. Because you want to be heard and you currently feel that He is kinder than I am. You feel a stronger protection with Buddha, but We are one and the same energy.

Q. My mother forced me to go to church. Why was that not helpful for me?

A. You came to Me through her church. Yes, your mother brought you there to worship Me. But you didn't want to worship anyone you didn't know. It scared you to be in a place where all the people were talking about sin and hell. You didn't want to be there because of your mother's fear. She made this her most important place, and your being baptized was what she wanted so you would be saved from damnation. That is what made you afraid, because you didn't know what that meant.

Comment: David continues his writing for support, and has many days in which he is free from anxiety. He moved away from the crowded city environment to Redding, California where he has met many people who are encouraging him to write a book about his story of "Stress in the Workplace."

Andrew's Story

Two years prior to seeing me, Andrew had received an award as one of the top trial lawyers in the United States. But, shortly afterwards, his whole world began to crash around him. He was chronically sleep-deprived from overwork and he unexpectedly lost a major multimillion-dollar legal case that created financial difficulties for his law firm. To make matters worse, his wife confessed to having an affair and soon left him. He found himself experiencing depression and panic. This represented a regression back to his traumatic childhood in which he had to deal with an unpredictable father who suffered from a Manic-Depressive Disorder. His physical and emotional condition had deteriorated to the point where it was necessary to place him on medical disability, and for the first time in his life, he had time on his hands to think. We were able to develop a rapport that was closer than he had ever felt with another human being, even though his life was filled with people that he called "friends" and who invited him to innumerable professional meetings and social activities. In his own mind, he had lost everything, and he began to wonder whether life had any meaning. I felt that it was safe to tell him that the only way that he would ever know the answer to this question would be to ask God directly. Although he considered himself an agnostic, he saw that I was serious and, because he had always been a conscientious student who never refused an assignment, he gave it a try. I suggested to him that he, initially, write down an honest appraisal of his life and his feelings as if writing to himself. I knew that he was second to none in preparing intellectual legal briefs, but I was impressed by the quality of the very feeling and articulate narrative that he brought to the next session:

> When I was in college, I read Albert Camus' book The Stranger. In it, things just happened as if actions were detached from the people doing them. I read some Sartre as well. This had an impact on me, not so much at the time, but later on in life. In the large context of my life, I realize that for a long time I have been empty of real purpose. Even my successful years were filled with only temporary and mostly material gains. Even what seemed to be success in my legal career, like winning trials for noble causes, I now realize were as empty as the financial rewards that came with those successes. A good reputation and a resume impressive

to others are in the same category. They are as meaningless as an obituary. Such things confer no real comfort because they come from outside and are only the opinions of others. When you're dead, they confer nothing at all.

I have always felt guilty when praised, mainly because it usually missed the mark. The praising individuals have no way of knowing what my true motivations were. As a result, accolades feel false and underserved. A thought that often haunts me is what am I doing anything for? Do I love my children because I'm afraid of what people will think of me if I don't? I feel like a selfish father with little skill and imagination, like an imposter who will surely be found out. Yet people don't see me that way, not even my children. While I care very deeply and think very emotionally about my children, I am inept at doing anything about it. The burden of thinking of something fun that isn't too much of a sacrifice or too much trouble is often more than I can handle. This is all part of the emptiness I feel in quiet moments. Trying to fill that void with women, my children, and activities, even worthwhile ones, does not work for me. I'm still empty when things are quiet.

I have prayed and no prayer has ever been answered, except by the ever-convenient response that whatever happens was the answer. Even a feeble-minded person can see that would be equally true if there were no God. Or is God like the Wizard of Oz, a little old man hiding behind the curtain, hidden from our view? I think not. But I also do not believe in God as a being who would allow me to twist in the wind with no possible answer to the question of why things happen as they do. Sometimes horrible things happen to seemingly good people. The criminal courts are full of atrocities committed against innocent children by awful people. Could these possibly be God's response to someone's prayer? Again, the brain God gave me tells me, "no". I am angry with God (if there is one) for giving me the mind he did that fails so completely at the task of understanding what to me is the most fundamental question of life. The answer to that question answers for me what is good and evil and what matters and what doesn't and what, if anything, waits for us when we die.

The most frightening thought I have is of dying. But my fear is not of the idea of dying. Often it seems like it might be a relief. My fear is that death is literally the end of my consciousness of everything. My consciousness is me. I do not believe that people are reincarnated as trees or butterflies or even as other human beings. Such an afterlife, to me, would be as meaningless as it would be if death were the end of everything. It would not be any consolation to me now to know that I might come back as someone or something else, even if

I could get my brain to accept such an idea, which it won't. The end of my consciousness is the end of me. The concept only has meaning to me if I am aware that I have survived death and continue to live in some way or other after death. If not, what's a life for? If that's not a relevant question, then nothing else makes any ultimate sense. We might as well be a colony of ants, well organized as a society, but devoid of any higher purpose beyond propagation and the survival of our species.

At this time in my life, changing careers, going through the pain of a divorce from someone I loved, experiencing the loss of loved ones, I am severely empty and deeply in need of some answers, not just therapy. Therapy can't touch these questions. Therapy can only touch the broken parts of our human psyche that we ourselves cannot see or understand.

I encouraged Andrew to continue his writing, but with the added idea that he was addressing a Higher consciousness outside of his usual awareness. He remained skeptical, but, nevertheless, he persisted until he came in with a result that he could hardly wait to share with me:

Dr. Pecci, I thought I'd write down my thoughts since my last reflections. As you suggested, for the past few weeks I've been waiting for some answers to "come back from the universe." For the first couple of weeks nothing came back. Nothing. I felt rather foolish. But then, like the scientists who were puzzled by the static they were hearing (the static later turned out to be radio waves from the big bang), words started coming out of me. It was if the answers were not out there somewhere, but were all around me all the while. All I did was look, listen and feel and then tell myself what I saw, heard and felt. I literally talked to myself, out loud, alone in the car. My questions for God were answered by me. Mostly the answers came back, "Don't you get it?" I created you to deal with all this. You will be judged by how you deal with it. All the decisions you make are yours and you are the judge. You answer only to yourself. When you answer to yourself, you answer to Me."

The answers to my questions didn't come to me, they came from me. All I had to do was say them out loud to give them reality. My life is a work in progress, a journey on a train. And, like a journey on a train, when one looks out the window, the perspective is constantly changing. At times I am in a tunnel. The view is black. I am afraid. Then light bursts the darkness and the scene is a beautiful countryside. But there is more darkness to come. So be it. There will be more light. But I know that both the light and darkness are merely projections on a wall and are not really part of me nor can they touch me. The light and dark are merely people and things that are part of that projection.

Things and even people only come to you when you let go of them. For it is only when you let go that anything or any one is truly free to be what it really is. When you hang onto something or to someone, a struggle ensues and you don't know what the person truly wants or what the thing truly is because you are trying to control the process. The realization for me at this point is a sort of calm resignation that consequences of my actions and most of what I see in others is not something I can or even want to control. After all, everyone is doing exactly the same thing, consciously or unconsciously trying to control or influence others. But for me, I now see that the path that will work to achieve what is good is to let go. I have the power to recognize what is good. I believe that everyone knows good when he sees it and that self-delusion is really not possible. No one can truly lie to oneself because that requires two people, one liar and one believer. No one person can be both, at least no one who is not mentally ill.

My task now is to separate from my own clutter and to allow things to be what they are. What freedom and what fun this is! I have met one particularly attractive and spiritual lady and we hit it right off. I'll tell you about her sometime. But to evolve spiritually, I have come to realize that the choice is a conscious one. Before, I have been evolving unconsciously and the result was confused and full of fear. Now, I feel quite free to let go of anger, fear and all the other destructive thoughts and to let my Higher Self, take over the reins of my personality. Plato thought no one could intentionally choose evil, because evil was harmful and no one would intentionally harm themselves. But that analysis ignores the role of time. One chooses gratification in the short run and postpones the real decision and the consequences for the long run. I believe that to really live life to the fullest, one must let temptations play themselves out in your mind so you can truly see what you are choosing in all its detail. Only then will your decision be a conscious one.

Needless to say, Andrew's progress was dramatic from this point, and he soon reached a new level of self-acceptance, professional success and a level of awareness and enjoyment of life that he had never experienced before. This has persisted and progressed to the present time.

Linda's Appeal for Help

Linda is an African- American teacher who has talent in working with disadvantaged children with special needs. She came to me because of her depression associated with a post-concussion syndrome. She had received a serious head concussion from a thrown bottle while supervising recess at a school where she was teaching. Her recovery period was prolonged and she was not getting the proper medical care that she needed. She was in pain from severe headaches and dizzy spells much of the time and could not understand why she was having so much difficulty convincing her Worker's Compensation doctor that she was unable to return to work. After several sessions, I suggested that there might have been a higher purpose to this crisis that was forcing her to make some significant changes in her life and the way that she was using her talents.

Q. Holy Spirit, please help me understand the pain in my head and body and how to let it go. Please help me to not attract negative people and situations in my life.

A. If you just relax and let Me be your guide you will know my presence as complete serenity in the midst of chaos. It will be a feeling coming from inside of you from the region of your head as a pleasant tingling sensation, an inner smile of recognition that I am here with you always in every situation and you don't have to worry about anything. This takes daily practice. I will help you as you consistently ask Me and choose Me. Right now you wish for healing and financial freedom. Remember no one can take any good thing away from you. You have to sit in the silence every day unhindered and unhampered, away from the maddening crowds.

You need time now for yourself to heal in a setting of green grass and flowers and trees and nature undisturbed for days. You will come away from this experience refreshed. Do not look to people to help. It will bring you into situations where the right spiritual people will assist you easily and effortlessly. All you have to do is to know without a doubt that I am here in you as God, the Spirit of eternal life, omnipotent love and infinite wisdom. If there is anything you want to know, be still and the answer will come from Me, your Source. Right now the proper medications and environment will help you to achieve this stillness. Later on you will be able to do this without the use of medications. Certain foods and vitamins will maintain the chemical balances in your body.

Your mental pace has to slow down so you can have focus and My knowing for you can come through as your infinite intuitive guidance. It will help you remember and do all things for the good of you and others you will help later on. Right now it is time for you to heal with the proper assistance. It will help you to trust those individuals who are truly here to help you.

Linda came to understand that this crisis forced her into making some major changes in her life regarding her career plans and to choose more carefully the people who were important in her life. It definitely forced her to become stronger in fighting for her rights and in taking better care of her health. She is still in the process of going through some important changes at this time. These consist of using spiritual support to turn away from the negative energies that she felt immersed in and to focus more positively upon the future changes that she now desires*.

* Just before publication of this book, Linda expressed a major shift in her attitude:

> "I was too depressed to get out of bed in the morning, and I suffered from frequent migraine headaches as well as chronic neck and back pain. I had lost all of my sense of self-esteem and became more and more socially isolated and withdrawn. However, through the consistent practice of writing to get in touch with my Higher Self on a daily basis I began to feel as if God's presence had entered my life. This inner experience has changed the outer perspective of everything that was occurring to me in the moment. With this change in attitude, my entire body has slowly released its pain and I now awaken each morning with a new sense of gratitude for the blessings I have all around me that I was not aware of before. My inner and outer vision was so closed off that all I could see was lack and limitation. Everything looked black. It was like walking through "the Valley of the Shadow of Death." Now every night when I go to bed, although outer circumstances have not changed significantly, I feel an inner warmth and a sense of reassurance that I do have support from a Higher level and that everything will work out for the greatest good of everyone concerned."

Christine's Experience

Christine is a middle-aged woman who came to me with a number of diagnoses given to her by previous psychiatrists and neurologists that included Asperger's Syndrome, Temporal Lobe Epilepsy, Post Concussion Syndrome, and Agoraphobia with Panic Disorder. These diagnoses had been placed upon her in response to her numerous physical and psychological complaints that had increased over time and that included paranoid thoughts, periods of "disassociation," mental confusion, an inability to communicate her thoughts and feelings to others, social isolation, and an extreme sense of guilt and fear of punishment for past "errors." She was taking numerous medications in an attempt to improve her concentration, reduce her fear, decrease her dizzy spells, and diminish her headaches. She also felt the need to take B12, B6, and numerous other vitamin supplements to ward off possible deficiencies.

Christine had a traumatic childhood that would fit under the diagnosis of "Disorder of Extreme Stress Not Otherwise Specified (DESNOS)." She had suffered paternal childhood sexual molestation, life threatening illnesses, and extreme invalidation of her feelings by both parents. I focused upon her strengths and learned that she had a talent in communicating with animals and especially with horses and cats. She explained that animals, unlike humans, are usually innocent and clear in their communications. She also shared that she had had some special "spiritual" experiences as a child when her stress became so unbearable that she "left her body." She blamed herself for not always listening to her inner guidance. She gave as an example the fact that she had given away most of her inheritance to a man whom she desperately wanted to believe even though she heard a "voice" warning her against him.

Of passing interest here, I will mention that she had a vivid memory of being a Jewish woman in the Holocaust who was painfully gassed to death when her German lover became disenchanted with her. She was reliving many of the feelings of that lifetime as if there had been no intervening time between her birth and that death. She felt stupid for having allowed herself to be naively violated, both then and in this lifetime, and was angry with God over this as well. She felt alienation against her Higher Self because of the seemingly needless and endless suffering she had experienced.

Christine was referred to me by Dr. Brian Weiss as a therepist who might help her. However, her fear and distrust of men was so strong that I felt the need to tape all of our sessions because she had a tendency to negatively distort every statement that I would make. She listened to her tapes over and over again to assure herself that I was not trying to deceive her for some reason. Even so, I had to allow her to frequently confront or to attack me regarding some remark she thought I had made in the previous session. Gradually, her trust increased to where she could quietly sit back and examine the lengths that her ego went through in processing all of my statements to her. To her credit, she was able to detect her pattern of resistances that commonly lie hidden beneath the conscious minds of most patients.

- I'm rebelling against needing you.
- I'm judging your motives behind your answers.
- I think that you have expectations I can't meet and you will reject me.
- I am embarrassed by and also afraid of experiencing my sexual energy toward you.
- I'm wondering whether you are coming from real caring.
- It doesn't seem possible that you really care about me.
- How can you like me more than I like myself?
- I am angry with myself when I feel like I'm blindly trusting you.
- I'm caught between wanting to argue and pretending to agree like I felt when I listened to my father as a child.
- I don't want you to think you know more about me than I do.
- I'm afraid that you will use what I tell you to control me.
- I don't want you to think I'm stupid or, even worse, disgusting.
- I don't think you completly believe anything I say.
- You can't possibly understand what it's like to be me, but you keep assuming that you do.
- I'm afraid that you are just going to put me into another negative diagnostic category.

- I'm not sure of the real meaning of every word you're using, but I afraid that there is some kind of judgment attached to every one.

Again, I appealed to Christine's talent in working with animals. I asked her to compare the difference in working with them and with people. She explained to me that animals don't have the kind of ego that humans have so she felt safe having a direct line of communication with them. I explained that this same fear is keeping her from communicating directly with her Higher Self, because the ego creates God in the image of other humans. She acknowledged feeling, at times, the presence of her Higher Self as a beautiful woman who was trying to reach her. Finally, after many weeks, Christine was able to sit down quietly one evening and communicate in writing for more than an hour of effortless flowing with her Higher Self:

Christine, my dearest, most cherished part of Me, you never will lose Me because We are one. You may go so far away in your mind that it appears hopeless, but our desire together will turn you and this feeling of loss around, and point you in the right direction.

You were not born with a fear of non-being – it was absorbed from your early environment and given to you by those who were not connected to Source, to God. Give those fears of annihilation back, or give them to Me. You will never be a non-being; will never be taken apart and scattered. You are whole. Yes, your way of learning this – your God-given worth – has been difficult, and the lessons seemingly harsh, so the sense of being punished has only increased for you over the years.

The dualities, the paradoxes were set up for you to come to see beyond them – to hold the seemingly polar opposites of your life in sight and then to soften your sight to see beyond to where all possibilities have life. You must give up wanting to be right for all the suffering you have experienced. There is a reason for it all. See how, in your adolescent stubbornness to define yourself, you set up a pattern of creating/allowing the opposite of what you really want in an attempt to assert your Self, your 'I'-ness. Now you can transmute that stubbornness into the determination to work on the opposite side of the scales – the positive, loving, light side where you are just as real – no, much realer by not having all the upsets, arguments, illnesses. Do a "180" as it were!

The Animal High Council wants you to know how honored and respected you are by them, in the way you delight in loving them, in how you acknowledge how much they give to humans and your world. So many on your planet don't understand about the potential that is just now starting to send up flares that must express itself. You recognize their consciousnesses as being akin to humans' - that can be elicited and nurtured into growing by validating their true natures as partners to the human race on this planet.

You know now, in the past couple of months especially, that you truly are healing, changing, your mind becoming clearer, a new sense of integrity to your body. As you gain more confidence in the knowing that you are not being punished for those emotions, thoughts, and feelings you were trying to hide inside your body (and which subsequently have caused many systems to go askew – from weight gain to brain confusion and amnesia). As these are leached from their hiding places, you will gain a clarity of thinking you have never had before, and which you will not shut off in the presence of men that until now it seemed necessary to do to save your life. Dr. P. will help you to complete the learning of seeing men differently, the learning of dealing with men on a one-to-one basis without fear of reprisals. Yes, you still have a ways to go – to learn what "being in your power" means – just know that it is done just as you are doing it, being there for moments, or minutes, or hours at a time first. You are right where you are supposed to be. We respect your pace; we just want you to be happy enough to willingly live out this life naturally.

You're right on course. Your timing is perfect. You have no "big thing" you're missing or not doing. We will continue to help you to relax into the now, as We have been these last few months. Together, We shall make your life easier. Often, you truly get overwhelmed by too many thoughts or feelings at one time, and then try to figure it out with your head, and then start to believe you really are missing something important, or else why would things not make sense if you had all the information or capabilities needed to be a normal human being. And so you're reminded of your prison walls and how you wake up some mornings wracked with the horror of knowing you can't get past yourself, past these limitations which have only become more well-defined and more pronounced as you've gotten older. So we want you to know We see you. We see you as the non-stop giver that you are. It is so much a part of your nature that you don't stop to think about it. For you, Christine, giving is who you *are,* not something you just do.

I'm with you always. I know your horrors. But you are always given a key, a clue, a trail of breadcrumbs to follow – have you noticed you haven't been destroyed yet, nor totally devastated? You are the heroine of your own life. You have great intuition but do not trust yourself or it yet. Ask for help in this area – it is a great gift given to you and a talent to develop. You use it so naturally in your work with animals, and can more than make up for your areas of limitation. Do not think for one moment that your differences in thought processes or learning abilities were or are a punishment for some past deeds or thoughts. It was agreed upon, and you will soon find your peace with it.

And now Christine – what you have dreaded – the answer to why we haven't been closer, why you haven't let Me be real to you. And then it won't be so bad, it will lift as we've already started to leach the anger from your body – the old calcified bits you hoped to hide forever and not let anyone see. Especially Me! I know the rage and bitterness you have felt towards me, and it does not appall me, nor does it cause me to think less of you.

Your momentary hate or railing against Me or God has not, and will not ever hurt Us in the way that you have experienced the hurt of being the recipient of other's hate. Of course, I forgive you, I understand where it comes from, the fears that generated it in the first place. You are fine and whole with or without it. With it, you feel separate and I wish otherwise for you, for Us. So I am gladdened by your asking for help to have it lifted. This great secret of yours shall have no more power over you – be happy in knowing this, for you were the one who made the choice and decision to bring it to the Light to be healed. And We honor you for that.

This will not be My one and only letter to you! The next time you start to do this again, only ask one question, then write what comes to mind, put your pen down, let yourself drift a bit in reverie, then more will come. The key is to relax – this is not a test. Pet your cat, and yes, it is me who comes through Callie. You know those times when her eyes get especially green and she gazes at you with such adoration and you see and feel the extra white light surrounding her. We have many ways to reach you! I say "We" because there are many others who are your cheering squad and who join Me in some of these explorations into your (denser) physical reality. It helps so much that you are so sensitive, in all the positive meanings of the word! Isn't that a paradox – that you have to slow down in order to be receptive to higher vibrations from our planes of reality!"

With love, affection and respect, your Higher Self.

The above was like a lecture being given to her, something like what occurs with people who call themselves "channelers." But Christine had no previous experience of channeling like this. I have found that some individuals who have had extremely traumatic childhoods are special Souls who elected this experience as training for a higher purpose in later life. In the psychiatric literature they are labeled as "resilient children," of which Golda Meier is often used as an example among many others. Shortly after this, dramatic events occurred in Christine's life that forced her to change her entire living situation and pushed her coping skills to the limit, requiring continual support from me and from her Higher Self through daily writing. The process is still continuing as her life is changing and she is beginning to accept the value that her past experiences have offered to the progress of her Soul.

Summary of Crises

The purpose of any crisis can be gleaned from a careful examination of the emotional impact it has upon those who directly or indirectly experienced it. The question is, "Where do you go from here?" The detailed treatment of each unique case is beyond the scope of this book, however the intent is to impress those who are dealing with a crisis situation that there is an approach that can shift their future direction from one of withdrawal, self-devaluation and bitterness to a spiritual transformation that results in extending oneself into the world in a more effective manner than before.

The statement made so often, today, that we create our own reality is misleading. Of course we can hypnotize ourselves in seeing or believing almost anything, but the surface consciousness of our mind is primarily an observer and does not have, directly, the power of willing outer changes. Many of the major events in our life have been predetermined at a higher level. However, in every case, the strong emotions of wanting and intention can seed our subconscious mind, stirring it into activity, and can reach out to our superconscious mind or Higher

Self to prepare the way for the changes and understanding that we consciously desire.

I have interviewed many women in their late fifties who still felt damaged as the result of being sexually molested in early childhood, and that this was still having a negative impact upon their lives. The emotional impact of the trauma of being betrayed and abused was held fixed in strong pockets of energy throughout their bodies and continued to radiate messages of rage, repulsion and the danger of being further victimized to their brains. Often these feelings are somatized into chronic physical symptoms. Conventional psychotherapy is somewhat helpful in bringing an acknowledgement of the pain to the surface and then encouraging an emotional release. However, there is a limit to what even extensive venting alone can do to bring about a permanent healing of the event. The traumatic experience of being violated continued to affect every area of their lives thereafter because they couldn't extract their identity from the experience.

What they needed to know, on a very deep level, is that childhood abuse, or any negative childhood experience, is never the fault of the child, even when their understanding of it never becomes totally clear. Your basic identity as a spiritual, loving and innocent being cannot be changed by any experience you have in the physical world. What is needed is acknowledgment, self-forgiveness, and a releasing of the incident through asking for God's help. The process need not be painful if the acknowledgement is clear and strong and the request for help includes forgiveness and self-forgiveness. There is only NOW, and the past is selective memory that can be changed.

It is difficult from the viewpoint of our ego to see tragic events as part of the natural course of our gaining greater wisdom. We have to accept the truth of this, without completely understanding everything with our everyday consciousness.

When we sink into the world of feelings we become immersed not only in the drama of birth and childhood in this lifetime, but in the group archetype, as described by Karl Jung, and in our past lives as well. Our current feelings and behavior including illness and health have their roots deep down in the hidden depths of our Soul. Some amount of self-inquiry and Soul searching, including past life therapy, can be very helpful in convincing us of the truth of this statement . The danger is that we may become stuck in all of this without guidance from a Higher Source.

PART III

A New Dimension In Psychiatry

This section contains aphorisms, affirmations and reinforcement of the essential truths in the earlier chapters of this book. Put it on your tabletop and turn to it when you need an emotional lift or some encouragement to make a shift in your thoughts in order to feel more positive about your life. Try to read one or two pages each day and, later, reread them again to more fully digest them. Interwoven within this material is Type "C" information that will gradually shift your perspective toward a whole new way of viewing your true nature and your perspective of the world.

7

A New Dimension In Psychiatry

The foundation of psychology in the Western world may be said to have its beginning in 1902 when Freud published his classical book on the interpretation of dreams. The time has come to raise his work to a new level, one that incorporates the ideas of Eastern mysticism that sees the experiencing of the true Self as the cure to all human suffering. Freud's contribution is not to be underestimated in that his seeking for the genesis of human behavior opened up a number of questions regarding the layers of the mind that are not accessible to normal waking consciousness. His theories, however, were not comprehensive enough to encompass all of the complex and wondrous aspects that comprise a human being.

Conscious life contains both emotion and awareness. Our brain is a computer that processes thoughts, feelings, the input from our five senses, and the learned beliefs that have no meaning outside of this limited 3-dimensional band of existence. Recurrent, repetitive thoughts from our Intellect can mold us into mechanical behaviors. Most of our thoughts do not really belong to us, but are merely echoes of the words of our parents and teachers. It requires practice to get in touch with our true thoughts and feelings. With more practice we can get in touch with our inner Self, independent of our ego's idea of the world.

Understanding What Life Is All About

It is essential to know the support that you have on many levels that you are not in touch with at this time. It would not be so difficult to experience and to use this support if you did not live in a society that denies your true identity and the existence of these unseen helping forces. Instead, you have been taught to use your body and your Intellect in ways that they were never intended to be used, and which leads to chronic overwhelm and stress. It is the reason why you think that life is difficult, when it was intended to be a joyful adventure.

When you are weary from your life's tasks, you may ask, "Where is the life force I so desperately need? Who can extend it to me?" This stream is absolutely available, constant, and flowing through every individual who has life. To breathe is to experience it. The only way through which love can reach anyone is in his own makeup. We don't have to journey to distant lands to find the fountain of youth. It resides as an exquisitely beautiful fountain within the Self. All we need is the belief system to turn on the tap. Seeking this from someone else is due to a lack of one's own inner clarity and always leaves the seeker looking for more.

Ask yourself, "Do I have value? Who am I?" Sit quietly and listen for clues. What makes you happy? What makes you feel good? What activity do you enjoy and resent interruption? Where do you wish to go? Learn the inner Self apart from everything else. Desire to see more of who you are. The quest for the Higher Self is but to know who you already are.

Earth desires are impossible to fully satisfy, such as a huge income, impressing your parents and friends, and accomplishing the many expectations put upon you by yourself. None of this satisfies the Inner Core. It is not uncommon for high-level executives to feel a vast emptiness inside. They have lost touch with their real needs and the awareness that these can be satisfied with little outer change. What is needed is a shift toward their insisting upon doing only what best serves their true life intentions. You have to stop trying to fill someone else's vision. Everyone's purpose is to allow energy to flow freely. Find whatever will bring you to laughter, joy, and appreciation.

Even infants are often put into situations where too much is expected. When they are unable to comply, an authoritative adult might impatiently imply to them that they are unworthy, useless, or a burden. The infant feels a need to be validated. When you have difficulty falling asleep, let your mind drift and begin speaking to yourself as to a child. Say things that will nourish your inner child such as, "At this moment you are cared for and receiving everything you need." "You are allowed to enjoy pleasure and fun."

Within three or four weeks a new drive for satisfaction will occur, and new situations and possibilities will become obvious. Certain experiences can become benchmarks that need to be expanded into all aspects of your life. Remember a moment of feeling briefly: "This is wonderful," or a time of feeling a sense of freedom with no criticism or implication that you were doing something wrong. When you lose yourself in any activity that brings joy, you are being your true Self. All those who dare to be themselves may initially feel a period of loneliness. There's never a crowd at the cutting edge. But there will always be companions as you begin to attract similar people to yourself.

At birth you were a beam of energy fully aware of all of your connections to other levels. From this place, you came into a 3-dimentional existence for the purpose of expanding. Conditions were set forth that were opposite to your essential nature. Early life experiences were often the antitheses of what you wanted and, so, contracted your energies. If you are experiencing intense restlessness and frustration, let this promote an intense questioning and searching in order to reach a rich goal, one that is satisfying beyond your present experience.

Awaken the damaged self. Not in defiance against something, but in an affirmation of yourself that redirects your energies. Say, "Feeling good is my intention for being here." "Feeling satisfied is why I am here, and why else?" Draw your feelings into everything that has been placed before you, saying, "It has a purpose, and one day I will understand it."

Beginning the Search for Inner Peace

What would it take to make you at peace with yourself, to feel self-accepting and acceptable to others, to become enthusiastic about your role in life and to know what it is you have to offer others?

The answer lies not in what you have accomplished, nor in what you have accumulated, but what you *are* now!

Life was meant to be simple. How has your mind succeeded in making it so difficult? How can you now attain a sense of balance through moderation and right thinking? You don't really have to do anything – and it is best you don't even try unless it is inspired by love. Treasure every moment, then let go of it, or you will not be able to enjoy the next. The challenge of this lifetime is to restore your true self from the definition the world has given to you.

Take the chip off your shoulder.
Let the world off the hook.
Stop thinking thoughts that make you dislike yourself.
Say, "I would rather feel good than feel angry."
Say, "I have come to heal the world, not to condemn it."

There is no learning without the realization of how you might have done things differently in the past. The purpose for learning is not to feel regret for the past, but to experience a new way for living your life now. See the past as a necessary experience to get you to the place you are now. However, with learning, you do not need to repeat it.

- Allow the imperfections you see everywhere around you to fulfill their purpose, even as the imperfect steps of an infant child who is learning to walk.

- Know what it is you do not want, and insist upon having what it is you do want.

- Do not make the mistake of trying to accomplish this by your efforts alone.

- Ask for what you want from your heart, with a sense of gratitude in the expectation of being heard and answered.

- Ask for the love to heal whatever family problem now causes you discord and grief.

- Strive to unite your conscious mind with the Higher mind that holds everything in place. Keep reminding yourself that all mind is one. See everyone as a part of yourself, deserving praise for his or her struggle to grow.

Every encounter between two people changes both in some way. Focus upon what you have to offer rather than what others can give to you or how they must change to please you. Do not identify with what you consider to be the inadequacies and egocentricities of your personality make-up. Accept them without defending them, while visualizing the direction in which you want to gradually shift. Take responsibility for your current negative state by acknowledging it, but not with guilt for the emotions or thoughts you acted upon in the past. These merely represented ways of reacting unconsciously. Guilt traps you because it demands punishment and thus continuously recycles a negative state. Rather, ask for help against the multiple influences that have kept you from being less than ideal in your own mind. You have a right to be free from all thoughts, emotions, and behavior that you dislike about yourself. Whatever you dislike about yourself is not the real you. A turtle does not complain about its shell, but a bird trapped under a turtle shell would be very unhappy. Focus on that small part of you which is innocent and vulnerable and holds the pure intentionality of a child. Allow that part to expand until it encompasses the entire you.

If you could hear a tape recording of the past, you would see that your recollections are primarily negative. How often do you make negative comments about anything? If counted, you might be surprised at the number of negative statements that you make each day. Take your thoughts out of the negative pool and find thoughts that bring you positive feelings and energy. Ultimately, it doesn't matter the subject, but whether it flows into the positive pool. Replacing negative with positive energy does not have to be about the same subject. It is that moment of energy and the direction it takes. Focus upon something positive in a series of "nows". You do not need to always seek the source or origin of your present discomfort. As you insist upon feeling good, uncomfortable body patterns will slowly decrease. There is always something satisfying to focus upon. This is the most critical exercise you can do to improve your health and your state of mind.

Finding Your Ideal Situation

There was a time when your present work situation was right, but now may be over-ripe for change. The situation has served its best purpose. It is time for a renewal, for pleasure and for joy. You do not need to assign judgment or blame to a situation in order to move on. There are multiple negative emotions that arise when people are not treated appropriately. Your only task is to see clearly what is best for you in the situation. You need not blame yourself or others. Let go of blame and bitterness. This will help you to bind to new situations. Clearly call to your attention the inappropriate behaviors of those about you without getting stuck in them. What do you now have the courage to do? Are you moving away from or toward what you truly want to do? The challenge of constantly considering new options and possibilities is an enriching exercise, whereas constant complaining perpetuates the very situation that you are complaining about.

It is not necessary to remain in a structure that is not serving you well. This may involve attending to many arrangements. But your Higher Self can assist you with the mundane aspects of your life. You are not stuck, but invited to see the situation differently. Dare to be "divinely selfish." It is an exercise in self-honoring. You have a right to have your basic needs filled in an environment of acceptance and respect. You must be true to yourself despite the upset it might bring to others. Unless you intend to bring harm, you will not bring them harm despite their squeals of protest. Neither should there be self-blame for waiting so long to make a change. Your own peace of mind is the most critical aspect of your life that you must focus upon. You have to constantly push your boundaries of comfort in order to be what you truly are.

A beautiful gem needs a good setting. All of the settings have value and a time of appropriateness. When one "life contract" is fulfilled, you are ready to move to a new setting. States of circumstances are related to states of mind. Make a declaration: "I am ready to do that which is better for me!" Express your intentionality. Make up your mind and the universe will respond. Become an observer of your own emotions and thoughts. We tend to automatically accept and act upon our thoughts and feelings without considering the arbitrary nature of their source.

Most people hesitate to make changes that will improve their life because they are afraid of what other people will think. You are not responsible for anybody else's happiness, nor can you harm anyone unless it is your intention to do harm. You are only responsible for your own life, because each person's life has its own journey. When you are doing something not out of love but out of duty, then you feel resentment.

You draw to you the lessons that you need to learn. And as you do learn, you need never experience these same lessons again. Until you understand how to embrace that which you judge to be painful, you will never have your energy centers free to tap into all the knowledge that is within you. An emotional transmutation must take place to change agony into ecstasy. It is the true art of alchemy, which creates molecular changes within the cellular structure of your brain.

Begin to notice in your daily activities that there is a constant interplay between you and a Higher level such as the special timing of events, the right thing happening to you, the right person coming into your life, etc. As you become a witness to this, you will recognize others who create confusion. You will notice where others are stuck, and be able to make choices more quickly. Do not be afraid of change. It is necessary to become that which you are meant to become. As you grow you will attract the best situations and partner. You were not meant to be lonely. You have written a happy ending to your story. Do not be afraid of moving into it! You can overcome your fear of other people by realizing that no matter how insignificant you may feel there is no one who would not appreciate your expression of genuine caring. Do not doubt this power you have. Begin practicing to extend it in the simplest of situations and even with people you encounter only briefly.

From the intellectual level some situations appear unsolvable. The Intellect feels pulled in different directions. The brain does not have any sensory nerves but is capable of experiencing "frustration pain." It's like an angry, hurt child giving up. A solution requires the multidimensional rearrangement of the material world, which the Intellect cannot do. But a Higher level can rearrange the 3-dimensional elements to create a solution. Thus, no person need remain forever in a situation that feels distasteful.

Asking the Right Questions
with Expectation of Answers

There is no question too easy, too profound or forbidden to ask. Begin to look with new eyes at old friends and relatives and focus upon the feeling and impressions you receive with an attitude of seeing them with new understanding rather than judgment. There is safety in doing this. Childhood has passed. It is now safe and appropriate to know what you know. Say to uncomfortable feelings, "This does not mean that I am doing something wrong." "What is not serving me and why am I uncomfortable doing this?" Ask for support and for answers. There is still a resistance to asking for help because it makes you feel indebted. God asks no price for your existence. It is time to direct your energies into doing what you most enjoy doing.

When you want something, do not worry about the way in which it will come to you. When you have a desire backed by a strong and clear emotion, you have already begun the process of manifestation. However, preconceived ideas of your limitations can limit the possibilities. Your body is like a neutral floppy disc that records the thinking of the mind. When you block your emotions, the body will create a discomfort to tell you to change your thinking. Whatever fear you experienced in your childhood, you will recreate over and over until you learn to accept it and release it through forgiveness. Fear is always associated with angry thoughts about someone.

The universe does not judge. It simply re-arranges itself to accommodate your beliefs. Whenever you are in a situation that does not feel comfortable – take some paper and make a list. On one side of the paper write down all of the positive things that you feel about the specific situation that you want; on the other side write down all the things that you think are not so good. I often ask patients who complain that they do not have a permanent love relationship to write down a list of the downside of a permanent relationship and, often, they are surprised by how many negative beliefs they hold about relationships.

Begin to take responsibility for your experiences. The moment you blame you do not take responsibility. This includes blaming yourself for making stupid mistakes, or for being so weak as to having fear in the first place. Pain is caused by judgments from the past. Whenever you believe that you are going to be hurt, resistance tightens your belly and closes your heart. Acceptance and surrender without resistance requires faith and trust. When you exercise surrender, you will allow intuition to flow in and through you.

Whenever you deny or invalidate something you empower it in your mind. So embrace with love what you want to change. Sit down and write a list: "This is what I desire to create". But take no thought as to how this will occur. Do not worry about the basic mechanism involved. Everything is merely a rearranging of energy patterns.

The steps to attaining what you most deeply desire are as follows:

1. Be sure that your motive is pure, then visualize as clearly as you can what it is you wish to be fulfilled. Picture its completion with all of the five senses.

2. State your plan in words and in writing as concisely and clearly as possible.

3. Keep reminding your Intellect that the ability to visualize is an attribute of God, and that it is God the Doer that brings it to fruition. Let go of all fear and doubt that your wish will be answered.

4. Read your desire or plan over several times during the day and then let go of it each time so that you do not hold the energy to yourself.

5. Do not discuss the fact that you are doing this exercise with anyone else unless it is performed as part of a group process. Do not even obsess about it to yourself because your Intellect might try to control everything.

6. Have no set time in your mind for results, except to know there is only *now*—just the immediate moment. See yourself as God picturing and directing. If the human side of you totally agrees to this plan and accepts it, there can be no such thing as failure because you are extending energy in an act of co-creation.

The Nature of Our Journey

Our journey is to follow a path that leads from littleness and limitation to grandeur. It entails the experience of pain, which is eventually transformed into joy. Pain results from the belief that you are not loved. But even more pain results from the secondary reaction of refusing to love or to receive it even when it is offered. Refusing to accept love can make you even more hurtful than those you now hold in unforgiveness because they did not know how to give it to you. It also creates a state of isolation, and a coping with the world through the Intellect that deals with concepts and not with love. The Intellect is constantly seeking for answers to problems. The reunification to God is the ultimate answer to every problem. But this can never be achieved by the Intellect. The Intellect keeps your upper chest and jaws tight to hold back the rush of energy from the belly where the inner child resides.

Love is an experience that might best be described as a joyful and sweet energy streaming through consciousness. Fear and doubt must be replaced with trust and receptivity to allow this to happen. You can begin by allowing yourself to be passively loved, and this can serve as a catalyst to your learning to extend it to others.

All of the answers to life's problems must begin with the reduction of fear and the permitting by the Intellect to allow the life Force to flow through the emotional center in your solar plexus. This is what is meant by learning to become one with Life. This is the ultimate goal that the Intellect's attempts to seek comfort can never reach. The key is the streaming of energy that must begin from the emotional center. Look at the joy of a child at play to understand this. But an even higher level of appreciation is attained when the mind acknowledges the Source as God who is sharing the experience with you.

Finding Joy in Life

What if you could view your life with the same attitude with which you might view your experiences while being on vacation and taking a tour of a foreign country? When you have trust in your guide, you have no responsibilities or expectations other than to see something new and interesting. When you come across a new situation, instead of feeling a sense of panic you might say to yourself, "How interesting. What is this all about? What can I learn from this that I can take home to tell my friends?" There is nothing you specifically need to do other than to listen for directions from your guide.

Our lives might feel more like this if we had faith in a Higher orchestrator who is guiding with care our every step from within. We can find the answer to all of our questions within ourselves when we overcome the fear of looking. It takes faith and the belief that you will be given the answers you need as you are willing to hear them. There is little joy or meaning in living an unconscious life. The pleasures are few and fleeting and often come at a heavy price. Without direction or purpose the mind become cluttered by its opinions and then becomes trapped in endless busyness in an attempt to create something meaningful out of the clutter. And eventually there will come an inner rebellion that results in tension, procrastination, paralysis, or depression.

Rather than passively seek comfort and escape from pain, we must actively pursue mental and physical nourishment and pleasure. Gradually, with practice, we begin to see the world as a mirror of our subjective reality, revealing to us from moment to moment who we believe that we are. The universe is composed of invisible energies in a continuous state of interplay and flux in the process of becoming. Those who are too wedded to their physical possessions or to their rigid beliefs suffer the constant stress of trying to hold in place that which is going through inevitable change.

Joy Is Your Intention Here

Joy is your intention in this dimension. Some people are afraid to be happy because it might be taken away. But there are always multiple resources for joy. It evolves out of the desire of the universe that we all move from one joy point to another joy point. The interpretation of events is what brings pain. In the story of "Adam and Eve," it was judgment that cast them out of the Garden of Eden. Humans have since become adept at categorizing things into "good" or "bad." And you experience whichever you tell yourself.

If you are not happy, ask for assistance in changing your judgments. The thinking mind only operates in terms of comparison and judgment. Everybody appears to be doing something wrong. But all we see are the superficial trappings associated with any type of behavior, which tells us almost nothing about the forces behind it and predetermining it. It is very difficult in our culture not to think in terms of judgment. The effort, in the beginning, to free yourself from negative thinking, can be small and gentle and yet bring about profound change. Buy a packet of seeds and scatter them about and notice how they can grow into large and beautiful things with proper nourishment. You need to pray, first, to overcome your basic negative state which prevents you from really experiencing happiness and joy, such as the feeling that you are unworthy of love, and all inner anger and bitterness about the past that needs to be healed with forgiveness.

In times of grief, disappointment, and sorrow say to yourself, "This too shall pass." This attitude allows doors to open. Write the ideal fairytale with a magical ending. This begins to set up and align the energies you need to receive. Set aside the rational mind in its attempt to solve all your problems. It has been trained to the point where it blocks the energy of the Higher Self to intervene. Speak out at least once each day, "Although I do not fully understand, I accept what happened and trust my Higher Self." This partnership energy will offer you guidance and sustenance. Answers will come depending upon your level of acceptance and, with this, your belief will grow that there is something in the universe trying to help you.

Many of the best answers that we receive merely point out our denials. We learn to pretend things are okay as they are. We learn not to see things that might upset us. We deny that our children or our spouse is not happy. We deny that we are neglecting our health. We tend to deny the things that we believe we have no power to change. But these are precisely the things upon which we must focus our attention. These are opportunities to exercise our power. You cannot look at something without changing it in some way. Just bringing your full awareness to the things that you are now afraid to look at will begin to change them for the better. If you have difficulty understanding the answers you receive, it is often because they contradict previous answers that you had agreed to accept and to use to run your life. Just by beginning to believe that you deserve more begins to put into operation the forces that will draw it to you. Begin to focus your mind upon what you want and not what you fear.

Make statements of declaration:
> I want to start being happy right now.
> I want to stop experiencing scarcity, fear, confusion, doubt, and guilt.
> I want to know the part of me I can love.

Confirm to yourself that you can get what you really want
> Whether you deserve it or not,
> Whether other people approve or disapprove, and despite any negative event in your past.
> You don't have to pay a price.
> You don't have to wait any longer than you believe that you must.

Willingness reawakens the expression of the Inner Core. It does not require preparation. It does not require suffering. It requires only willingness.

The universe is in a state of constant flowing. When you are flowing with the stream without resistance you are totally powerful. When you are fighting against the stream, you are totally powerless, regardless of your determination, convictions and persistence. Some people are afraid to relax because they believe that they are turning the wheel that keeps the stream flowing.

Make Happiness Your Goal

A good question to ask God is, "Why am I not more happy?" It is hard to believe that life was meant to be a joyful adventure when we see so many unhappy people. An exciting adventure may contain obstacle courses, but never impassible barriers. Most people do not set happiness as their primary goal, and many people feel undeserving of it. Yet you were created to increase God's joy of existence. Every life contains a book worth reading.

One of my surprising discoveries, as a psychiatrist who has interviewed thousands of people, is how low the level of happiness is in our relatively affluent society. You can confirm this for yourself by the following mindtrip:

The Happiness Test

Close you eyes and visualize an average day in your home when you were about ten years of age. Visualize your mother standing in the kitchen or the living room. Beside her is a tall thermometer that reaches from the floor to her head with ten numbers. At the floor, the number 1 indicates her being depressed to the point where she dreads to get out of bed in the morning, while at the top, the number 10, indicates her being in a state of total elation and happiness. Where would you place the meniscus? If you look beyond her facade, it would be rare to see it above the halfway mark. The average person is actually below it.

Let's contrast this to a puppy dog that was unwanted and sent to the pound to be exterminated. This is the ultimate rejection. Then a little boy or girl comes in and says, "Mommy, I want that dog. Please buy it for me." They take it home, feed it and pet it. How long will it take before that dog has a happiness level of eight or nine?

Why is there such a big difference between animals and people? It isn't so much what happened to us in the past as what we tell ourselves about it afterwards. Healthy animals do not obstruct the ever-present energy of the universe that surrounds us all by worrying about the past or the future. Animals have a natural faith in Mother Nature while humans depend upon their Intellects for security. It requires the energy of negative thinking to suppress happiness, which should be our natural state. Depression needs constant negative thinking to feed it. Life needs only the acknowledgement of the love that sustains it.

Everyone has skewed perceptions and beliefs that become incorporated into feelings. Truth can come only when you begin to honor your true inner feelings, initial impulses and desires. This means overcoming your fear of wanting, asking, and knowing. Try to sense Truth bouncing off your chest. Happiness comes from within oneself. Everyone's primary task is to transform the feelings of helplessness as a child into the power of a mature adult. All growth involves looking back at the past with regret or guilt over past errors of judgment. But rather than let this drag you down, it can become the impetus for a strong

resolve toward a new beginning. It is like the turning of a coin.
NOW is all that matters. A new awakening dissolves the past.
On a higher level it actually changes the past since the past
consists of isolated memory, much like a dream, from which
you can make a fresh start at any time. So become open to
whatever answers you get, believing that the truth is always
much better than you think.

What Keeps You From Being Happy

- You can never be happy if you have to wait for other people
  to be happy.
- You can never be happy if you think you must earn or
  deserve it.
- You can never be happy so long as your Intellect is too busy
  to let your inner child play.
- You can never be happy until you realize that your main
  purpose is to be happy.
- You can never be happy so long as you have enemies whom
  you don't want to be happy.
- You can never be happy until you know God wants you to
  be happy.
- You can never be happy until you understand the meaning of
  creative expression.
- You can never be happy so long as you depend upon your
  Intellect to solve your problems.

B.J. Skinner, the renowned psychologist who founded Behavior Therapy, once wrote, "Here I sit in my living room. I am in good health. The sun is shining outside. I have attained recognition and respect in my profession. But I am not happy."

What would it take to make you happy right now? Would a phone call announcing that you had won the lottery make you happy? How about a realization announcing that God is your real Father and that He loves you and that He wants you to play and be happy, and is waiting for you to receive His love?

Viewing the Earth Experience
From a New Perspective

A lifetime of less than one hundred years is not even the blink of an eye in terms of eternity. And, yet, we tend to become concerned about what we must accomplish during our life and spend needless time worrying about others or become upset by external circumstances that will not likely be remembered by the turn of the next century. We do have a specific purpose that can have lasting value long after our physical body has completed its stay here. What we learn here we can take with us, and whatever love we give to others they can take with them also. This entire stage upon which we now play out our life experiences with those who chose to be here at this same instant in time, to engage with us in greater or lesser ways, will all be soon cleared up for the next generation of Souls to play out their own drama.

When I worked with children in play therapy at Mt. Zion Hospital in San Francisco, there was nothing of lasting value to accomplish in our activities in the playroom other than our own connection or communication that somehow enhanced the value and the self-esteem of the confused or rebellious children that I would became engaged with in play activities. Many of them showed surprising artistic and creative abilities, but what was more important was that they learned new patterns of relating that was more productive than their previous dysfunctional patterns of rebellion and defiance. What really mattered to them was my consistent caring and love, which those who appeared to be helped the most were gradually able to accept. Then, whatever we had done would be put away and the room would be cleaned up for the next child who was scheduled to come.

Similarly, there is nothing of lasting value that can be accomplished here on earth except that which leads to the growth of our identity and its connection to the Soul. This can be done in small ways that have immense value, but that cannot often be measured in earth terms. Our predetermined status, talents, or fame are merely different vehicles for particular experiences. It is often the player who holds the center of the stage that becomes the most tragic figure, the most gifted that often struggles with heavy emotional turmoil, and even the rich and famous experience their own disappointments and grief not unlike your own.

We Are Like Lost Souls on Planet Earth

1. We do not honor what we think and what we feel. This is because this was not honored in our childhood.

2. We are so hungry for contact that we make the body a symbol to fill our needs.

3. Fear keeps us imprisoned in isolated cells. We make contact with others with our bodies, but not with our inner selves.

4. We underestimate the despair in others and make them our judges. But they cannot tell us who we are because they do not know who they are.

5. We have made a silent agreement with our parents to stay asleep. (Breaking this agreement would heal them, as well as ourselves).

The agony we experience on planet earth comes from the conflict that keeps us split from our Self. Guilt, fear, and self-judgment keep us from looking within where the true connection must be made.

> We hate what we don't deserve to love.
> We seek significance in insignificant ways.
> We cling to what we cannot hold onto.
> Love has become something that carries pain.

Grief has become one of the main emotions that brings people together.

Our schools focus upon our left-brain, like a microscope, examining the world of illusion, while our right brain becomes silent. We feel powerless because we have lost sight of our Source of power.

Does all of this serve some higher purpose? Perhaps . . .

We experience limitation in order to appreciate the unlimited.

We experience insignificance in order to appreciate our grandeur.

We experience the hells we create to learn better how to use our gift of consciousness.

If you are now sufficiently acquainted with pain, loneliness, frustration, and fear you are ready to move on to something new and wonderful. We are all somewhat afraid of change and the unknown. But we are much more uncomfortable holding onto our fears than any discomfort that change would ask of us. There can be nothing lost, and a life to be gained in taking another look from a new perspective.

What World Do You Live In?

There are two worlds, the world that God created and the world that you see, which is covered with fear. The concept that we all live in a different world is difficult to understand because the world that each person sees appears so real. The following example may help you to understand how important your mindset is in creating your world.

Let us suppose that a friend had talked you into seeing a horror movie called <u>The Creature From the Dark Lagoon.</u> Although you are not particularly interested in horror movies, you finally agree to go. The movie opens up with a scene on a sandy beach with children at play, laughing, and splashing water at each other. The camera pans to a scene on a grassy area next to the ocean water where two teenagers are lying down beside each other giggling and playfully necking. There is the sound of a heavy beat in the background. Your initial impulse might be to close your eyes because you can't bear to see what is about to happen to these naive children. Why aren't they paying more attention to their surroundings? How could they be so unaware of the danger around them? You decide to leave because you do not enjoy the tension you feel.

You tell your friend that you would rather see the movie that is playing in the theater next door. It's a Walt Disney movie entitled <u>The Happy Days of Childhood.</u> Your friend finally agrees and, as you are seated, you see a sandy beach with children at play.

There is a lot of laughing and giggling in an atmosphere of happy frivolity. Nearby there are two embracing teenagers lying in the grass and engaged in playful antics. The background beat sounds somewhat lighter. Your mood might now become one of nostalgic chuckling.

What makes the difference between this second movie and the first one? It is precisely the title. What kind of movie are you now living in your current life? It is likely one that was created by the background atmosphere of your home environment. If it is a horror movie, then there is no room for security or happiness because that's the exact timing when tragedy usually strikes. You would be afraid to relax or to care too deeply about anything or anyone. In fact, there might likely be a fear of loving because that would be the set-up for a real tragedy. There is only one solution. We must continually upgrade our current world view until we are comfortable and safe with our role upon the stage of life.

Help is Needed to Overcome
the World Illusion (Maya)

Let me try to describe the problem that prevents you from
accepting the concept of direct communication with God. When
the connection is finally made, it suddenly becomes so obvious
that you wonder how you could ever have denied it. It brings
the feeling of an interconnectedness with all of nature, rather
than the sense of a solitary self you now experience within a
physical body.

You have a conscious Intellect that becomes programmed to
serve like the default settings on a large computer. You have a
Subconscious Mind which contains the emotional imprint of
every experience you have had in a physical body, recorded in
symbolic language that includes subliminal, psychic, and
archetypal information that rarely reaches consciousness, but
sometimes comes up in dreams. You also have a Higher
Consciousness that retains your memory of your oneness with
God. And you have a brain, which does not initiate thinking,
but is merely a keyboard upon which all of these levels of
consciousness play. The brain can be easily programmed to
deny, repress, inhibit, override or greatly over- exaggerate the
significance of any input it receives.

It does not take a scientist to know that you cannot test reality
with a flawed instrument. Yet you are constantly testing your
reality with an extremely flawed set of instruments. Let me start
with your eyes. You currently believe your own eyes without

question, and yet they have been programmed to see what is not there and to deny what is there. You live in a virtual reality module in which you can learn to manipulate the instruments of perception and can continue to become engrossed in the experience. But the better you are at doing this, the more you become lost in it.

What I am suggesting is that you must question all of the conclusions that you now make as a result of your perceptions. That is a hard thing to accept. But how else can you begin to deprogram a hypnotized subject? A hypnotized subject, given a post-hypnotic command, will comply with it and then vehemently defend his behavior even though he has no recollection of the motivating source behind his actions.

You are currently living in a virtual reality and under a false identity. So long as you remain focused upon your world of virtual reality you remain limited to its program. You do have a Center, deep within, that remembers your true identity, and there is also a Voice that is trying to convince you to turn your conscious focus within and upon that Center. You can begin to make the transition relatively smoothly now if you wish. What is involved is an unplugging of your input connection to the outer world and to plug it in to the input of your Higher Self. It is not as difficult as you might think. All it requires is a small amount of willingness. Unfortunately, most people have to reach a state of anguish or despair before taking their egos off of the "handle bars" and trust going into automatic pilot. It becomes, then, like a death of sorts. But what is on the other side is Life.

The Detachment Syndrome

Perhaps you are among the many young or older adults today who are going through a state of what might be called "existential despair" over the repetitious routine of your life, a feeling that you find difficult to explain because others may see you as fairly successful and relatively stress free. Yet you feel driven by an inner urge to find something that is desperately lacking and that is compelling you to keep searching. The timing of your finding this book is not accidental.

First, there needs to be an understanding of the connection between that portion of your Higher Self that decided to take up this experience and your current sense of identity or the personality that is now experiencing it. Your 3-dimensional experience has been uniquely designed in all of its physical and energy aspects. Your sojourn here has immense value even when it seems to make no sense. Whatever you experience contributes to the knowledge of energies in other dimensions. One aspect of the purpose of your present lifetime is to experience the opposite of your true nature. This ultimately leads to a greater sense of beingness and to a larger sense of Self. You may have always felt a sense of isolation for two main reasons: 1.) The connection to your Higher Self has been denied or forgotten, and 2.) Most of the people around you were going in a different direction or were out of harmony with your energy.

However, it was essential that you be brought to a place of high desire before the answers you seek can be received. Sometimes it requires a severe illness or a life-threatening crisis, or the sense of frustration and loss of direction such as you might feel at this stage in your life. There needs to be an intensity of questioning to the point of despairing. When you realize this you will know why everything that has come before makes sense and has purpose, as does your present state of dissatisfaction with the answers you now have. In your past you experienced an imperfect sense of connectivity with your parents, family, and friends. This is because you have chosen the antithesis of what you most desire. This motivates the drive to a higher level of questioning, seeking, and understanding. It leads to a feeling of differentness and a sense that you can never fulfill your true desires. We might label this *"The Detachment Syndrome"*. Thus, despite any recognition of your achievements you still feel this aloneness because you were reaching for something higher than the individuals around you could offer at the time.

All social beings intensely crave a connection to others with whom they can resonate at their level. Lacking this, there is an emptiness that is not easily described nor understood. It is felt inwardly as pain that others do not see and do not even understand. The friendships that you seek will come only after you realize that inner understanding is what is most important. Inner understanding allows you to respect and expand your consciousness in beautiful ways. It is a process that moves in continuous waves of questioning that brings new understandings.

There will always be periods of discomfort, impatience and, especially discouragement. But a higher awareness of the whole process can bring you comfort as you pass through these challenges. You are being constantly guided toward the understanding that you need whether you realize it or not.

Humans tend to look for answers through their thinking mechanism as it perceives and examines patterns and seeks to find a purpose in them. Your thoughts and your desires do have power, but your Intellect is not the mechanism that will bring them to fruition. Your Intellect is merely a translator of the clues being given to find the doors that are being opened. There are not many true seekers, but they do exist and they yearn for a partner whose thoughts more closely match their own. The following is an exercise that might help to bring this about.

In our culture, there is a tendency to ignore the Heart Center – the connection to love – which is the most directly connected to your Higher Self. Spend some time each day focusing upon the heart center and reiterate: "I feel lost, but I choose to be guided beyond what my thinking mind has to offer." Think again of the time when you felt an outpouring of love for another human being. Try to describe that feeling. Was your body filled with a sense of vitality and aliveness? Did it make you fully present in the now? Were all of your senses enhanced so that even the surrounding environment seemed more beautiful? This is what the energy of love flowing through you does. Most people are afraid of love because they do want to feel the sadness mixed with anger and pain if that person should leave them. But you must know that this other person is merely a catalyst and not the source of your good energy. It is the energy flowing within yourself that gives you the greatest joy. The danger is in interpreting this feeling of joy as a vulnerability to pain and something to be avoided.

However, you can use that experience as a touchstone: "That is what I want to always experience as a human being." This was not merely a temporary experience to expose your vulnerability. You can always have this again in your life in which you experience the fountain within yourself continuing to bubble. But it is important that you realize that the outer world cannot bring this to you. Therefore nothing in the universe can take it away. The source of your good feelings are always your own inner alignment and connection to your core Self. That which flows directly from your Higher Self brings the "peace beyond all understanding." Your craving for a meaningful connection puts you on the cutting edge of the very few who seek the completion of the circulation of the energies of Higher Mind through the body and back out to all of creation. Your body then becomes an instrument for the expression of universal love on the physical plane.

One of the problems you may be experiencing is the doubt as to whether your life has any real purpose. But just by your existence you are inputting data into the total consciousness of all existence. You are valuable as a human being regardless of

what you are currently doing. All activities are only a vehicle
for learning. If you find something to do that is enjoyable, that
is fine. If not, as you patiently appreciate yourself more you
can ask for guidance to the activity that will give you the greatest
satisfaction. The only measure is the satisfaction that it brings
to you. Do not let society decide what is the most important
thing you should be doing. Joy is your goal here. As you come
into the experience of joy, love energy and the feeling of being
connected and, in practicing that connection, you will be
contributing more to the universe than you can imagine in
worldly terms. You will also be contributing to the possibility
of others to make similar questions and to find the same answers.
You help other people most by your example, by being someone
genuinely pleasant to be around. So whatever makes you happy
contributes to your value.

Here is an exercise to do when you are experiencing a sense of
detachment in which you find it difficult to even ask questions
or to know what will give you pleasure:

1.) For 15 minutes, be quiet and focus upon the Heart Center
in your lower chest, saying to yourself, "Body, mind, and
emotions relax."

2.) Allow your secret thoughts and fears to come to the
surface. The feeling of not being able to connect is based
upon statements you made to yourself in early childhood.
These statements are now directing your life program and

must be released one by one. These are statements such as: "I can never have what I really want." "I can never be good enough." "I am physically or mentally lacking in some way." "I am not a likable person." Etc., etc.

3.) Substitute these negative statements with a new conviction of will: "It is time to open up to spiritual guidance." "Guide me toward what I need, what I desire, and to knowing what would make me truly happy."

4.) Then, like blowing on a dandelion, let the seeds go out in all directions to find what you desire. Within even one month you will begin to notice a difference.

The Inner Battle Waging

There is a great battle waging within each of us that is not unlike a plague, which we often choose to play out upon the stage of life and infect those closest to us with our grievances and self-hate. The wise man knows that the battle is his own to win or to lose and refuses to turn his eyes away from it or to project it upon others. Neither can he turn to others for help because only his own judgment of himself can decide the outcome. We all have a different form of insanity in which we must learn to slowly separate the lies from the truth.

> Everything we feel about ourselves that is unwanted is not true.
> Every thought that encourages attack to solve a problem is a lie.
> Every critical attack you make upon another, you believe about yourself.
> Hate can become like an addiction that offers a temporary relief from guilt.

You are the God of the universe within. There is no other battlefield. Our task is to create within ourselves a place of peace or be trapped in a hell. Love is the only emotion that brings peace. Are we willing to forgive ourselves and all of our grievances for inner peace? It is as easy, and as difficult as that. It can be accomplished in an instant merely by a decision. Ask God to help you to make that decision. It must be made in the

NOW where the past becomes a dream without meaning and only your present wish has any power. When you can drop all guilt, judgments, and burdensome expectations, all there is left is peace.

Changing the Past

Replace guilt and regret over the past with the understanding that it was a necessary path for your growth. Review the past whenever the impulse to do so arises. Record in specific detail what you would now do differently.

- When you were withholding of love.
- When you were preoccupied in pleasing others.
- When you were being selfish in the way you were seeking approval..
- When you missed opportunities for giving.
- When material things and possessions occupied your mind.
- When you gave your power to others at a heavy price.
- When you neglected to do what was needed or what was right out of fear.
- When you were insufficiently considerate of others.

- When you were blind to the facts of the situation.
- When you blamed others for your weaknesses.
- When you wish you had given more.
- When you were too weak to say "No" or to take more responsibility for your life.
- When you were lazy, self-indulgent, or lacked self-respect.
- When you abused the caring of others.

Just your acknowledgement of the above is a signal of the beginning of your awakening consciousness. Positive changes will now automatically occur.

Handling Anger

It's not what happened to you in the past that's a problem but what you are doing to yourself now. Your head is so filled with tight knots over perceived abuse that you don't know what to do to relieve the pressure.

> Don't get busy.
> Don't look for something to eat or to drink.
> Don't call a friend for sympathy or for comfort.
> Instead, put everything into God's hands: "Holy Spirit change my thoughts about this." "Help me to see this as a chance to grow and to affirm my invulnerability."

Have a talk with yourself:

- I refuse to let this change my energy vibration.
- I forgive all players involved and put their future in God's hands.
- If I have a further role to play, let me feel the nudges, give me the courage to do something different than to follow my old pattern.
- Help me to remain focused upon my heart center so that neither fear, anger, nor guilt will influence my thoughts, my behavior, nor my speech.
- I pray for those who have upset me and for those who now give me concern.

- Regardless of the present situation, let all of my future behavior be loving.
- Help me to remember that I am now an adult and not a child.
- Help me to see the positive options.
- Help me to trust my heart.
- Help me to open up and to become more alive instead of closing off, shutting down and hiding behind a wall of denial and forgetfulness.
- I will behave as a kind and loving being, no matter what.

Some infants need a transfusion at birth because of blood incompatibility with their mothers. See this change in thinking as an exchange transfusion. Positive statements will begin exchanging negative thinking for positive thinking.

We need to Stop Running From Ourselves

All the things that our ego is running from are the very things that we need to prompt us toward our goal of self-discovery.

> Confusion leads to new questioning.
> Fear compels an exploration of our unused resources and talents.
> Adversity forces the will to stand strong.
> Sorrow softens the protective covering around our heart.
> Grief exposes the vain strivings of the ego.

What are the things we really need?
What do we need to appreciate the person at our side?
What do we need to accept the treasures of the moment?
What do we need to trust the direction our life has taken?
How might one discover that inner place of calm, free from all upsets?

> By desiring nothing,
> By envying no one,
> By accepting everything.

This is the secret of getting out of our own way and following without resistance the lead of our Indwelling Self.

> It's all right to be angry.
> It's all right to be depressed.

It's all right to be skeptical.

It's all right to feel jealousy and hate.

It's all right to hate yourself or to feel sorry for yourself.

It's all right to believe everything is too hopeless to change.

You don't have to wait to change any of this before you talk to God. In fact, there is no way that you will ever be able to change any of this in a permanent and significant way without God's help.

It is difficult to understand how God can help because He does it in a way that your Intellect does not understand. The answer is not what your Intellect thinks should be done, but nevertheless leads to the results that you really want:

To feel safe,

To feel capable and whole,

To be happy, and

To experience love.

Learning to Forgive Ourselves

Everyone seems to be making mistakes and doing many things wrong, but they can't help it. As you awaken and grow in consciousness, some guilt and regret about the past is inevitable. But as you forgive others you will forgive yourself. The more unenlightened a person is, the more likely he is to be self-righteous. Self-righteousness is a stuck place that impedes the growth of new awareness. The one thing to remember, no matter how confused or anxious you are, is to be kind. That is a simple yet important rule to always follow.

You want the future to be different from the past. The one thing that holds you back like a "tar baby" stuck in tar is unforgiveness. Accept it all as an experience you needed to get where you now are. Be more aware of the guidance available to take you to the next step. Both anger and fear indicate a lack of connection to the Helper along the way.

What you can never know is everything that you are now struggling so hard to learn: to make sense of the intimate intricacies of the world of illusion.

What you must not forget is the heart's delight in new discovery and the joy of the full experience of mind and body in playful activity.

What's real is the heart's longing for love, the seeking of your own significance in the kaleidoscope of the world, and your longing to return "home."

If you would bathe in the healing fountain of inner peace, look not to your parents who knew only ceaseless struggle. Look neither to the established institutions of learning nor to the books which line your shelves waiting to be read. Rather, look to nature and learn from even the simplest creatures around you about the wonder and the pleasure of the moment. The creatures of the forest do not labor to prove what needs no proof; namely that you are loved as an integral part of the grand plan of creation. Labor only to cleanse your inner garden from the weeds of lies that merge with the Truth, and that make for you a most difficult task which the lower animals can do so easily – to release all of your holding places and to trust God. Learn the law of the mind lest Life be forced to teach it to you: That which you fear you create and then it will haunt you as you have taught it to do. That which you hate you attract, what you fight you become, and there is no escape from what you are running from. Your mind will tie it to you so that you will see it in every direction you turn. And so your efforts to escape feeling despair will force you to live constantly within it.

Your Life is Like a Dream That You Can Change

I once taught a class on dream interpretation. A young woman arrived late as other students were sharing their dreams. She raised her hand to say the following:

> I was driving my car and didn't realize that it was running out of gas. I had to pull over on the freeway and try to find someone to help me. A handsome looking man stopped and, initially was very polite but he soon began making a crude pass at me that made me a little frightened of him. I began to wonder whether I was going to be a candidate for a gruesome story in tomorrow morning's newspaper. Just then, a police car pulled up and this guy took off.

Knowing this student's background, I plunged in with my interpretation: This dream is telling you that you have to begin to take more responsibility for yourself and not to keep expecting your prince Charming to come up and rescue you. As in the past, he turns out to be someone that you need to be rescued from.

She interrupted me with, "Oh no, this was not a dream. I was trying to explain why I was late to class. This just happened to me on the way here."

I felt my face flush a little with embarrassment, and then resorted to what my teenage son used to say to me when I caught him in a predicament, "So what?" Then I thought, "That's right; so what!" It's all the same. It's difficult to believe that everything in your present situation is interconnected with meaning as if by a magical formula. But that's what happens in dreams. Every object and person has special personal meaning to the dreamer. If that is true in our dreaming sleep state, why can't it be true in our waking sleep state? Since then I have made an effort to see the uncanny truth of this. On some level, all of the energy around you, in every given circumstance, is in a dynamic resonance with your own energy. This makes you a very important person, the star of your movie, be it sit-com or drama.

Are you not the creator of your own dreams? Why else does dream analysis reveal so much about you? In what way does the dream that you had last night reveal a reality or truth about you? Why should the elements within the state of conscousness you are in right now be less meaningful than the elements within your dreams? Your conscious state is not unlike a dream from which you cannot awaken, but which you can make more beautiful. You have an amazing power to attract, create, or enjoy what you wish.

In your dreams, other people you meet can be interpreted as representing an attitude, one that you, yourself hold, or an aspect of yourself either disowned or incompletely integrated into your energy structure.

Every thought you entertain in your head affects the dream in some way. The energy in which you enter a dream is the energy that affects the way in which all of the participants in the dream will express themselves.

Learn to Raise Your Attitude

Our thoughts make judgments which, in turn, create fixed attitudes about ourselves and the world that are quickly conveyed to others. People's attitudes are what draw them together or push them apart. Attitude is the major element that influences the duration of any relationship. It could be said that attitude is the only difference between a devil and a saint.

Attitudes are created by our thoughts. There are thoughts that are uplifting and create attitudes that raise the vibration of our consciousness and result in happiness and success. There are other thoughts that create judgmental attitudes that depress our consciousness into seeing only problems and frustration.

The following diagram catagorizes attitudes as being either "Ascendant" or "Descendant". In the ocean of consciousness and emotion, much of the world is struggling like catfish scavenging through the mud on the button and competing for the biggest or shiniest looking rocks. Since we are all spirits by nature, negative emotions function like balast to keep us at the bottom. As an enlightened few begin to detach themselves from the rat race of materialism and competition, they begin to rise like bubbles. Bubbles from the lowest depths enlarge rapidly as they rise to the less pressurized higher levels toward the surface. Finally, they will break through the top and become one with the All. This is the path that everyone must eventually take.

Appreciate Your Consciousness

Consciousness is a gift that must be used in order to grow. It can be a joy to experience, especially when you sense the connection to your Higher Self who is assisting you in your growth. It is of greatest benefit when you know the right questions to ask and when you are willing to accept the answers that usually lead to a gradual shift in the way you interpret your perceptions. It means putting together the various parts of yourself that are now in conflict or shut down. We all want acceptance, a feeling of worth, a sense of purpose, and the joy of full partnership with our Creator. You are now ready to get the answers that you wanted when you were a child. All problems are problems of misunderstanding, of feeling helpless when, in fact, you have the potential for limitless power when you are receptive to tap into it. When your thoughts are in alignment with your Creator, you are filled with appreciation and love.

God offers you a place of rest and peace. Trust him to write the script you want for your life. See it as your life's main purpose, and value the enjoyment of sharing your own unique experience with Him. Let exuberance, passion, and curiosity energize you. Let the desire for new experiences, for mastery, discovery, and creativity guide you. Let the expectation of connection, sharing and love inspire you. Be as a child in an amusement park with a loving teacher or parent at your side. Survival is never an issue. Decisions are always prompted by your heart. Time is relative and a gift that makes adventure possible. Your mind and your memory have been limited in order to make new discovery possible. Getting lost and facing imaginary obstacles is like playing peek-a-boo.

There is no greater joy than the discovery of the power of your will to direct your thoughts into raising your awareness to higher and higher levels of knowing. Make God your constant companion. There is no pleasure He would deny you. There is no experience you cannot have. There is no desire that will not be fulfilled.

You need never be envious of others. You do not have to strive so hard to be admired or to be important. You are not in competition with anyone else. If you are not wealthy because you failed to invest your money in the stock market or in real estate it is because you were not prompted to do so. You now have all the money you need to accomplish what you need to accomplish. If you have not accomplished important things in you life like the actors, authors or politicians who are receiving accolades on television, it is because your energies were not meant to go in that direction. You are experiencing now exactly what you need to experience in order to learn what matters and what doesn't matter. What people who really care about you want from you is your awareness. Appreciative attention equals love. There is nothing of any lasting value you can accomplish during your brief stay here other than the expansion of your consciousness, which is what "Soul growth," is all about.

Do not judge your life by comparison with other men who made great social changes such as Henry Ford, the men of genius such as Einstein, talented musicians or artists such as Mozart or Rembrandt. Those who have explored the wilderness, scaled high mountains and created new inventions that changed the direction of social activity or scientific thinking were all inspired specifically to do exactly what they volunteered to do before birth. Their lives were not necessarily happier or freer from disappointment, contention, and grief than your own. Your own perseverance against childhood limitations and your silent personal inner struggles to understand yourself and to find a sense of worth are equally noble in God's eyes to those whose achievements were publicly chronicled and acclaimed by society.

Every person, through the daily living of their lives, contributes to the continuous evolvement of the universe. Your experiences are unique, filled with problems that create questions, deep strivings of dissatisfaction, and limitations that necessitate struggle, challenges to survival, and failures or rejection that throw you back upon the resources of your essence Self.

It is in your moments of greatest despair and lack that perseverance for its own sake is your greatest contribution to the energy matrix of human consciousness. If you are lost in the desert heat and know that you will expire, but that with an effort you can walk ten more minutes before you die, then do it. Let your state of consciousness in persevering be your contribution to universal knowledge.

You are filled with dreams, aspirations, and unusual talents that often have no avenue for expression. It is not your Intellect but your heart's desire that will open the door. You must ask to be used and to cultivate patience. How does a godlike being who denies his own right to exist find truth? Notice the struggles of all those about you and learn from your attempts to help them. Give when the opportunity arises. Learn the value of your caring and attention. Do not judge yourself by a timetable of things accomplished. The test of a true man is the control of his spirit and his mind and to follow with courage the prodding of his inner voice.

Rest frequently, and expect that the energy and inspiration will come to guide you through the next challenge at hand. Some of your greatest moments of inspiration, connection and success occurred when you thought you were too tired to see the next person waiting for your help. It is at such times that you allow your Intellect to relax, to forget the goals you have set, listen quietly for guidance and allow the magic of your meeting to follow what direction it will. No person can sit in the presence of another without both changing in some way. Listening carefully for the voice of that part of the person who "knows" can become an empowering experience for both.

You cannot be your own guide out of the problems that your blind spots have created. Only God can do this. An attitude of stubborn independence limits the help you are able to receive. This attitude is probably the cause of your problem in the first place. To accept help means giving up your resistance to receiving it. It means being willing to acknowledge that you do not know what to do and cannot do anything without help. The test of your understanding is whether or not you experience perfect peace. A person guided by illusions and filled with inner conflict cannot be at peace.

See yourself as born over each moment, with the past only a dream, and no concern for the future, focusing entirely upon the consciousness of now. Take this moment and pretend there is no such thing as time. Remember, the connection of your consciousness to God is now. Consciousness is existence. Consciousness determines time. Your consciousness is independent of the illusions of the world. Once you understand this you are free.

Your consciousness is free of the five senses as well. Practice expanding your sense of conscious awareness beyond the five senses. You'll be amazed at the sense of power that comes from this. Then ask for guidance to the next moment of now as a newborn child who knows nothing about the world. The world seems to be changing all about you, but your consciousness is stable and is either expanding or going to sleep. Seek the remembrance of eternity. Practice seeing your brothers and sisters as free from the past. Help them to appreciate this instant in time with you.

Your Will Can Change the World

It is difficult to believe that you are Holy and that your own will, working through a mind distorted by fear, has created the world you see. Your will has the power to invoke a radical change of mind to see a world that serves you so long as you sustain it with love. The thoughts you entertain in your head must come from your Higher mind that maintains its connection to God and not from your little mind filled with fear.

God wills that you enjoin His will in the act of co-creation for its own sake. There is nothing you cannot do and no problem you cannot solve so long as you embody the energy of love.

Do you wish to perform miracles to impress other people or, conversely, only yourself in your increasing ability to cement your relationship to God?

How simple, yet so difficult, are the lessons to be learned. I remember trying to teach my young daughter how to whistle. I demonstrated the technique by whistling a simple tune, but I had difficulty explaining what she was doing wrong when she could not produce a sound when she pursed her lips. I remember saying that it was too easy to explain: "You just do it." She replied, "It's the easiest thing in the world when you know how, but the hardest thing to do when you don't." Everything takes practice. You must practice more the joy of extending yourself rather than maintaining the lifelong pattern of protective withholding. There is someone you can reach every day in a special way if you will take a few moments to think about it. Whenever I hear that a friend has died, those lost moments suddenly become very vivid to me.

To enjoy the experience of increasing the expansion of your consciousness to higher levels is associated with the opening of the heart. There comes with it a sense of being surrounded by smiling faces and all the barriers to creative activity removed. All of the elements that are needed appear miraculously, and smoothly fall into place. The mind creates through an unswerving will coupled with desire. Physical effort is smooth, tireless, and unhurried. Information comes as needed. Decisions are intuitive and without conflict. Activity is enjoyable and prompted by inspiration. There is a sense of playfulness in the belly coupled with a sense of higher service. Commitment draws helpers, doors miraculously open, and there is an unimpeded flow of energy. Resources become available as well as time. There is not so much the sense of doing in terms of work, but the joyful participations in co-creation.

The Importance of Self-Inquiry

During the course of self-inquiry we must never forget that we have a will that determines at this given moment what direction the course of our life shall take. We do not need to deny the fact that a real material world exists as part of a Divine plan. But the way in which we experience it is almost completely a projection based upon our fixed beliefs and the feelings that we are experiencing in the moment.

Anyone who has seen a stage hypnotist cannot help but be impressed by their ability to convince subjects to see things that are not there or to behave in ways that are totally incongruent to their usual personalities. For example, I have seen a construction worker who was told that he was a female belly dancer, and he put on a very persuasive demonstration. Even a post-hypnotic suggestion can be triggered by a word or a gesture and the unwitting subject will be compelled to carry out some ludicrous behavior for which he might later try to invent some rational explanation for doing.

So what do we do with this morass of information? First we must focus upon the consciousness of our inner or observing self, disconnected from all thinking, feeling, or need to act. Observe your surroundings as a newborn child, saying to yourself, "Who is this that is seeing?" Or "What is that who sees?" Ask for help in expanding your awareness beyond your perceptual limitations and then invite the Helper to settle in your heart and to help you to experience the Divinity in everything including yourself, independent of all past memory.

Our affirmations are more powerful when they expand upon our previous reality rather than deny it. For example, everyone feels to some extent, "I am unworthy, not good enough, and incapable of accomplishing or achieving what I would really like to achieve." Instead of denying it, add, "Humility forces me to acknowledge that this was largely true of the past, but with Guidance I can now do anything." Affirm your guilt and self-discontent, and then put it into the category of necessary learning and move on. As we grow we need to learn to look at our previous state of unconsciousness without criticizing ourselves.

Remember there is a positive opposite to every negative. You must constantly seed your subconscious mind with the thoughts you want to keep: "I have been stuck on one end of the barbell feeling lonely and that nobody loves me, but now I am going to extend myself to the other end of the barbell and experience the polar opposite." The small part of our conscious awareness with just a small amount of focused concentration can expand through the "don't pass" firewall into the subconscious mind to implant joyfulness, love, and forgiveness. Expansion is the only way out of depression. Unless you remain consciously aware of yourself you will mechanically create your childhood circumstances over and over again in your workplace and in your home environment.

Be True to Your Own Motives and Feelings

In all of your efforts to seek respect and love, remember that your main concern must be to become acceptable to yourself. This comes from giving rather than taking from others. Ask yourself, "What is it I truly have in myself to give to others?" Your questions to God should ask for clarity regarding this.

As a child we have transient feelings, thoughts and experiences that are generalized into beliefs that contribute to our identity in the world. Each thought and each belief has a life of its own with the desire to sustain itself. With time there is the stronger and stronger tendency to lie to ourselves rather than to change our minds. These early thoughts, perceptions and feelings interlock into what psychiatrists have come to recognize as "neurotic complexes. Most of these are unconscious conflicts with what we have surmised are the fixed beliefs and attitudes of our parents, teachers, and our social structure. From a relatively early age they color all new experiences by correlating everything with the past. This was noted by Freud and labeled as "transference." It is like driving your car through the freeway of life by looking only through the rear view mirror.

Most crippling is the blocking and suppressing of our creative and spontaneous energies by labeling them as "bad." This puts us in constant conflict with our own nature and hence, with ourselves. Thinking soon replaces feelings, and our behaviors adjust to a mechanical social model of conformity and competitiveness that has no relationship to our indwelling Self and what really constitutes a human being. In addition, each person has his own individual personality type and temperament that promotes its own perspectives and makes each person's life a unique and personal experience even within a given social structure. But, in any case, there is rarely a lasting sense of peace because the many "primitive" energies and needs must be held in constant check by the Intellect that, in turn, has its own inner struggle between conformity and nonconformity. Eventually, our personality is held in place by a fixed attitude about the world that is somewhere between the two extremes of resignation and defiance. In either case we lose sight of the fact that we ourselves are the creator of the outer world.

Constant communication with God expands your emotional awareness of your life journey as if you are sharing it with God. It helps you to recognize repetitive patterns and states of mind that you might wish to change. It prepares your mind to receive new ideas. This is when the voice of God can become a positive and uplifting influence, bringing with it a sense of personal validation and the encouragement to change one's perspectives to a more cheerful outlook upon life. The answers that come are only useful if you are willing to put aside your present perception of yourself. Your Higher Self is constantly trying to reach you to upgrade your perceptions about yourself. But it requires desire, faith, and a willingness to listen.

Do Not Give Up On Your Desires

Everyone tends to think that their problems and experiences are unique and different from others. In one sense they are; however, we must recognize the commonality of guilt, resentment, anger, fear, helplessness, self-hate, aloneness, lack, confusion and alienation. It is the result of our whole society being cut off from their true Self where their true power and sense of purpose resides. The earth plane is now covered in a cloud of negativity and fear, requiring both faith and perseverance to remain happy. What makes you happy is the key to feeling alive. Think back into the past to a period of time, no matter how brief, in which you were actively engaged in doing something that made you feel happy, preferably an activity in which you were being creative and without any sense of rush or anxiety over performance. Use these memories as touchstones.

There is a misunderstanding about desires; those that benefit and those that block progress.

Your desire for Truth will guide you to it.
Your desire for material gain makes material things more
 important than you.
Your desire for power denies your own God-given power over
 all things.
Your heart's desire will teach you your life's purpose.

Appreciation differs from desire. Appreciation of beauty opens your heart. The handiwork of craftsmen and blue-collar workers who put their hearts into their work deserves the same admiration as does the music and prose of gifted musicians and writers. Appreciation brings a sense of camaraderie with your brother and sister Souls and can become a source of inspiration and bonding between races.

Nourish Your Inner Child

Your inner child may have been taught at an early age that its energies were a problem, unwanted, or bad. This was an invalidation of the life force itself. Then its energy became scattered, and that was accepted as the norm.

Happiness and positive emotions are cohesive energies. They actually can assist the Intellect to think more clearly. As these energies are freed up there may be a sense of unease over the inability to understand and to predict the result. There needs to be the understanding that these energies are intrinsically positive and to trust them.

The purpose of inhabiting a human body is, first, to live fully the earth experience. So try new things, going places, and experiencing new situation as fully as possible. Next, donate your joy of sharing your expanded self to add to the lives of others. The barriers that now seem impenetrable to move through can be seen as opportunities to break through with the assistance of others drawn to your energy. Ask only, "What things do I truly love to do if I were free from all limitations and obligations? It is never too late to do those things you always loved to do, and are free to make the choice despite the attitudes of those about you. Children often feel that they will be rejected if they revealed what they really felt and thought. Thus, most reveal only the comfortable, superficial layers to others without even being aware that they are withholding an important part of themselves. People limit their selection of friends and new experiences when they are uncomfortable with themselves and limit the expression of their core energies.

Put a hand on your belly and say things that will nourish your inner child, such as, "At this moment you are cared about and receiving everything you need. You are allowed to enjoy pleasure and fun." Within three or four weeks a new drive for satisfaction will occur, and new situations and possibilities will become obvious. Certain experiences can become benchmarks of what you are, that need to be expended in all aspects of your life. Remember a moment of feeling briefly, "This is wonderful," or a time of feeling as sense of freedom and no criticism for doing something wrong. When you lose yourself in an activity that brings joy, you are being your true self.

A child at play is an example of unimpeded energy in motion, motivated by a fully present desire for new experiences, curiosity, and mastery. Thinking is replaced by spontaneity and aliveness. The joy of discovery and of new experiences, even the happiness of sharing this with a pet dog, is all done without words and without the need to understand anything. Attention without thought is the only way to be in the NOW. A child that has been traumatized by blame or verbal abuse by a parent can be detected by his hesitancy and self-consciousness as he surveys his playing field trying to avoid any actions that might lead to the pain of the past. He is viewing life through the lenses that his parents put before his eyes, which dramatically diminishes his aliveness.

Explaining God to my Daughter

My young daughter once asked me, "How can I believe in God? I can't see Him anywhere."

I replied, "Close your eyes and imagine that you are seeing a little girl playing in the park. Give her a nice dress and pretty shoes. She is wearing her long hair in neat pigtails. Place her near a lake where she can feed the ducks. Give her a big bag of popcorn. Maybe you would like to give her a puppy dog to pet. Think of a lot of other interesting things you might like to put around her, including some other children, and then relax and enjoy her having fun exploring the park. As you do this, she becomes more and more real to you. Her expressions become spontaneous and you can actually enjoy her experiences along with her as she swings on a swing and slides down a slide. Now you might send a young woman to greet her and to tell her that you had created her and that you wanted her to know that you are planning an interesting adventure story for her. By making contact, she could ask for things she wants, like a pony, for example. She begins looking around but she can't see you. She doesn't believe the woman. However, the moment you stop visualizing this cute little girl, she will disappear. Now end this exercise by pulling the little girl into your heart and feel her warmth there. So God is seeing you all the time or you wouldn't even be here. But you will never just disappear. He will make you as happy as you will let Him before He pulls you back into Himself."

God, Tell Us About Children

When you speak of children you are addressing the naked heart of God. Here we have innocence seeking only good, unconditional love yearning to express itself openly, and joy as the main motivation to put the body into activity. The world is alive, and every tree, every bumblebee, every breeze brings a message acknowledging their own aliveness and their invitation to participate in the symphony of life.

All too soon this is corrupted by fear, which comes from the adults about them who would teach them to place meaning upon the things that have no meaning in their own world. They must learn about competition, and right and wrong, and the work that must constantly be done if they are to survive. They learn that somehow, in the scheme of things, they are bad and must constantly struggle against themselves in order to be good. And they must be sure to learn the ways that measure whether they are being good or not. They must constantly compare, and try to please, and get good grades, and do what's right which means remembering all the "no's" and the "don'ts." They must learn to become serious, which means hiding feelings and to collect all the substitutes of love which they hope can someday be cashed in for happiness, which means approval.

In the beginning, when it all seems so overwhelming, they are tempted to go back to that grassy place near the big tree, watching the butterflies visiting the flowers and try to hear again that voice of nature which once was so friendly and made them feel so happy, but which now they must learn to ignore and will one day forget they could ever hear. Yet, many still keep, deep within the secret places of their hearts, the dream that someday the adults will come and learn to listen too, to that gently voice that says, "Everything that you are struggling so hard to find you already have."

Get into the Dance

The universe is in a constant dance of energies of every dimension and every vibration flowing in every conceivable way, but always in harmonic patterns that create exquisite sensations, colors and sounds. Everything is always changing, everything is very transitory, and nothing is the same twice. Less than 10% of these energies unite into a configuration which we call matter. Quantum physicists have been amazed by their own calculations that indicate that there might be more energy in the space between matter than in matter itself. The mind seeks security in trying to maintain permanence. It needs certainty, predictability, and a feeling of control over the status quo. Can you understand why it might see problems in every direction it looks, especially when the awe of childhood was replaced by a lack of trust and fear? We need the Helper to take us by the hand and lead us back into step with the dance.

The Answer to the Three Questions

The secret is so simple that any description of it only makes it more complicated: You don't try to be less jealous, less anxious, or less selfish but, rather, you put yourself into a state of consciousness where such things have no relevance. It involves a massive letting go and a total surrender to the purpose and plan of the Creator. There is no thought of how much to give – you give everything, all the time. It means maintaining under every circumstance an attitude of acceptance, gratitude, praise, and love. It means going beyond physical appearances and seeing the God-self in everyone else. Everything is all being taken care of and you do not have to become concerned in any way with the results of any action by yourself or of anyone else. You must only have the courage and the will to carry out your role, to read the lines assigned to you this very minute. The drama unfolds before you, conducted by an intelligence you cannot comprehend. Yet you can be and are part of it as you choose. Every moment can be a peak experience when you know the answers to the three questions which instill so much anxiety in humans:

1. Am I safe?

> **Answer:** "There is no death, no needless pain, no sudden attack of harm or tragedy that is not in the restraining hands of the loving Mother-

Father-God who directs all things toward the infinite security of ultimate awareness."

2. Can I cope?

Answer: "What is is, and what shall be shall be regardless of your fears of coping. Relaxing the mind attunes one to the silent cues that lend direction to your will. Humiliation and failure are only concepts that must be repeatedly experienced in order to recognize their irrelevancy. Give what is given you to give and the results will always be the most that can be attained within the given situation."

3. Who am I?

Answer: "One with the All. The eternal Witness. The Enjoyer. The obedient Child and the loving Mother-Father-God blissfully united."

The Final Steps to Attuning to Your Higher Self

Once you have become aware of the presence of a Higher Self you many begin to turn over the reins of the Intellect to this "automatic pilot" to direct your life. This appears difficult because you have been led to believe that the Intellect really decides your behavior from moment to moment. Quite the contrary is true. It is the past that determines your behavior and predetermines your perceptions. You also believe that only by the disciplined activity of the Intellect that your most cherished ambitions can come true. But this only results in stress, impatience and, ultimately, frustration.

1. Awaken one morning with the intent of turning the Counter to zero. Everything begins from now. Each day is seen as a rebirth. Your old self is "Under New Management." This means no guilt for the past even when acknowledging the mess you created under the old management. Acknowledgment corrects the past. There is also a general amnesty for everyone who was involved with the old management. At the same time, everyone is given a fresh chance to support the new management.

2. Begin a gradual surrender of all physical resistance of the animal emotions of survival fear, anxiety, anger and defensiveness in combating the inumerable obstacles and the individuals who appear to stand in your way. Rather there is a sense of harmonious flow with the environment, and momentary

delays become opportunities for peaceful introspection and inner attunement.

3. It is essential to maintain a constant willingness to not only remain aware, but to remain aware of being aware. With this comes an ongoing appreciation to the universe for the gift of your existence. There is no sense of hurry, as time seems to expand from your increased valuing of now. Gradually you will become a witness to your life experience and begin to see that it follows a definite plan.

4. Stop thinking, stop talking and begin to listen to your inner Core. Your Higher Self already knows your innermost needs and will fill them all as you become more receptive to listening. Shift the constant attempts of the Intellect to make all decisions into an inner dialogue with your Higher Self as you put all judgments and conclusions on hold as you ask:

What do you want to show me?
What is the meaning of this experience?
How can I see these apparent difficulties another way?
How can I improve this situation?

5. Practice maintaining the thought of God in even the most simple of tasks that you do. Gradually your body will, literally, feed upon the energy of Presence. Only then can your mind begin to discard its weeds of impatience, irritability, resentment,

and negative thoughts. Become an expression of positive energy in thought, action and speech:

> Search for positive things to appreciate.
> Expect positive things to happen.
> Look for beauty and the exquisite expression of life that
>   appears everywhere.
> Look for something that is positive in everything, and never
>   utter a word that does not have a positive sound.

6.   Work toward maintaining a certain "feeling" that comes from shifting the focus of your consciousness from the head to the Heart. With this comes the awareness that your heart center is the major focus of Divine attention and love. Enter each new situation from the heart center. In this way, your stored emotions of fear, unworthiness, guilt, and limitation can be transmuted and dissolved by the higher energies of love and joyful anticipation. Gradually you will begin to notice the little "coincidences" and "miracles" offered to you each day by a benevolent universe.

7.   Maintain a warm belly. This is the home of the inner child that wants to play, to bond with others, to explore and to be creative with the material substances that the earth experience provides. It is filled with effervescent energy that brings a sense of exuberance to the rest of the body.

8. Contemplate frequently upon the direction you wish to go in understanding, happiness, fulfillment and the kind of people you wish to invite into your life. Each life has a special purpose. You will know yours when you begin to listen to your heart's desire.

9. Practice co-creation by making the desires of the heart into resolutions that you carry through to completion. See every crisis as an opportunity to discover a new talent or strength. Look for opportunities to heal others by giving them a vibration they can resonate to. See everyone as potentially serving your ultimate purpose. Provide every opportunity for them to do so.

10. Cherish all of the Souls who have chosen to share this brief interlude of existence with you. Never be jealous of their possessions, their fame, or their superior physical beauty. Spend more time in the appreciation of what has been given to you. It is not what you have, this fleeting moment in time, but what you make of it in service to the eternal Good. This book, coming into your hands, can give you more clues toward fulfilling your life purpose than anything any other person has whom you most envy. Have compassion for those people who are trapped in an angry personality configuration. They will not offend you while you remain free from fear.

11. When unexpected things happen, be curious about the outcome, as if watching a movie. Remember, your personal

survival is never an issue. Dare to lift the veil of darkness you put over the world in early childhood, and allow everything around you to become fully alive once more.

12. You are now empowered to set the tone of every new situation you encounter by your own vibration, unassailable by outer circumstances.

God, I am weary of studying and trying to comprehend the meaning of the sacred scriptures in order to adjust my life to them. It is so hard to follow all of the dictates and rituals of the religious life and to remember all of the advice given by the teachers that you send to guide us along the path Home.

Yet, all the teachings of all the Holy Ones that I have sent to you can be summed up by these two words: "Remember Me."

*All that you really
need to know
is that
it is now safe
to love
as much
as you want to.*

Index